WHY I FIRED

MY BOSS

&

HOW YOU CAN DO SAME

Kenneth Ogbebor

CONTENTS

Preface
Acknowledgement
Dedication
Introduction

Part One: WHY?

1. You are fired! 1
2. Security threat 8
3. Are you having fun yet? 18
4. Easy does it? 25
5. Raise the roof 32
6. Who wants to be a millionaire? 45
7. Retire rich, retire young 50

Part Two: HOW?

8. Think like a CEO 61
9. Working hard vs. working smart 79
10. Best kept secret 94
11. Time and money 103
12. Yes I do 126
13. VIP only 139
14. Common mistakes entrepreneurs make 150
15. New world order 164

My aim is to take you off the unrewarding resume and cover letter; hire and fire cycle, while putting you on the road toward becoming a self-sufficient, financially free employee or business owner, and creating a life that gives you a real shot at the success you deserve.

PREFACE

It takes an entrepreneur to harness other factors of production in order to achieve the desired end of the production process, which is either a tangible product or a service. Without such a rallying point, all the factors of production will be juxtaposed as mere potentials dotting our economic landscape.

To convert potentials into tangible reality requires a prime mover. The entrepreneur is the prime mover that drives the gears of production. More often than not, this prime mover is the weakest link in the chain of production. Any marginal improvement in the quality of the entrepreneur leads to a quantum leap in the enterprise. This book is primarily focused on building the entrepreneur that builds the enterprise.

It does not matter what field of business you are operating in, or employed in. It does not matter what background you come from or what constraints you have to work under. It makes no difference what terrain you have to run on, or what resources are at your disposal. It is irrelevant whether you are climbing the corporate ladder or you own the ladder and the ground it is standing on. It is of no consequence if you are self-employed, an employer or unemployed; if rightly equipped, you will make a success of whatever you do, wherever you do it and no matter what you face. Equipping yourself with the right tools for the journey gives you a real shot at making a success of your endeavours.

While some may be born into fortunes, entrepreneurs are not born but made. The making of anything involves methodical processes which can be mapped and replicated by those who know.

Those who said "what you do not know cannot kill you" got it wrong. "What you do not know may be killing you, and the only way to live life to the full is to acquire relevant knowledge.

"We Shall Not Cease From Exploration And The End Of All Our Exploring Will Be To Arrive At Where We Started And Know The Place For The First Time"

ACKNOWLEDGEMENT

Writing a book is definitely team work. I cannot take all the credit for what this book has become but I will take the blame for everything it is not.

I have had great teachers and mentors all my life, and if I have come this far, it is because I have stood on the shoulders of these great men.

I appreciate my best friend and my wife, Marilyn and my awesome twosome, Bibi and Queen Esther.

Nobody takes care of family, like family! My thanks go to my parents, Mr. and Mrs. Ogbebor, my siblings, Ernest, Lorreta, Susan, Augustina, Juliet, Eugene, and their spouses, you guys are the best.

To all who helped to review the early manuscripts, Okhaide Akhigbe, Kezia Oyerekhua, David Dauda, Joshua Egba, Igwe kalu, please accept my heartfelt thanks.

To my editor, Chizoba Uzodinma, thank you for a job well done and God's speed.

To Pastor and Pastor (Mrs) Ikenna Okeke, and members of The Father's Church, you have been an awesome family to me. To Dr. Mon Igbinosa and the Gospel Outreach Ministries family, there is no place like home.

Thanks to Igwe and Nana for the cover design concept and Emmanuel for the cover photo.

To my publisher, Mr. Humphrey Akaolisa, thank you for making this dream a reality.

To all my friends, too numerous to mention, you have made life's journey a lot more beautiful.

To Dr. Myles Munroe, my mentor extraordinary, I miss you in time; I will see you in forever.
And above all, to Jesus, the Author and Finisher, I give all glory now and forever, Amen.

DEDICATION

This book is dedicated to everyone who has felt the desire to find true freedom.

This book is dedicated to the potentials trapped inside every man yearning for expression.

This book is dedicated to everyone who has had their back broken, their hands blistered or their knees bruised out there in the fields of life, yet are still in earnest pursuit of the dreams in their heart.

To every entrepreneur who is out there in the trenches pursuing their dreams and to every employee whose heart is yearning to unleash the entrepreneur trapped within.

This book is dedicated to the pursuit of greatness within, in spite of our conditions, antecedents or precedents.

This work is dedicated to the birth of the greatness in you.

INTRODUCTION

"He who knows how will always have a job, he who knows why will always be the boss."

Ralph Waldo Emerson

Most of the books on our shelves either deal with the "why" or "how" of people's issues in life. This leaves us with an incomplete paradigm. It is like having a map without the reason, purpose, or "why" for the journey. Or like knowing the "why" but lacking in skill, expertise and capability or "how" to navigate the journey.

This is a compendium of the why and the how of personal fulfilment, advancement and success in firstly, the mental sphere of your life and then in the economic and all other aspects.

Whether you are an employee, self-employed, an employer of labour or planning to become an employer, this book will help you see the destination (vision), chart your course (planning), set your sail and adjust if necessary (change), so that you can avoid the rocks and pitfalls (problems), profit from ill winds (failures) and make quantum leaps from good winds (success) till you arrive at your desired destination (purpose).

You will arrive at your destination in style. You will enjoy the journey, have time to smell the flowers, share precious moments with friends and family, make a meaningful contribution to our world and leave a legacy for future generations, when it is all said and done.

One pertinent question that should be addressed from the onset is; "should every one become self-employed or an entrepreneur?" The safe answer would be "No, some people have to be employed". Who said? That may be the status quo, but who said it has always been like that and who said it has to remain that way. The only constant thing in life is change. As such, employment dynamics, corporate culture or economic systems are changing. If we do not understand the change, stimulate it, control it, things will indeed change but we may be short-changed with the result. This book is not about not working for anyone, it is about "working for yourself", being your own boss. It is about questioning your hand me down answers if you have to and finding new questions whose outcome profit you. This book is about understanding the rules of work, the rules of money and the rules of life. Everyone may not become self-employed in the economic sense of it, but everyone has to think like a CEO, a self-employed person, a business owner or an entrepreneur.

To understand the meaning of "Firing Your Boss", we just have to look at the reverse scenario of being "Fired" by your boss. When your boss fires you, it simply means that you cease to work for your boss, so you owe him no obligations and in like manner, he owes you nothing in return. He cannot give you tasks, determine your schedule, order you around and in reverse you will not be paid or enjoy any benefits from him. In like manner, when you "Fire Your Boss", you cease to work for him. You are on your own, you own yourself and you can truly start to work for yourself. "Working for yourself" is simply what it is. You may be literally employed by someone or some company and yet be working for yourself. It depends on how you understand the rules of the game and how you choose to play. We will explore this concept of "working for yourself" in a later chapter as it applies to self-employed people as well as employees.

When people hear the phrase "firing your boss", some immediately think the idea is to resign their job and become self-employed. You can "fire your boss" even though you are still in the traditional paid employment and being self-employed may actually buy you more bosses if you do not do it right. You may not fire your boss today, this week or this month, but you do yourself a whole world of good if you start thinking and planning towards it.

This is not about a status change or a title change or job change. This book is about a paradigm shift or a mental shift. Wherever you are right now or whatever you do, thinking like a CEO or an entrepreneur is the sure path to the winners circle.

For the Bible says, "... as a man thinks in his heart, so is he". Ultimately, life is a self-fulfilling prophesy. Your life will go in the direction of your most dominant thoughts. Some people may get one or two lucky breaks in life, but these "breakthroughs" can become "breakdowns" if we are not equipped to manage them. Our success or failure in life will be according to the thoughts we hold of ourselves.

Entrepreneurship is not just about "what" you do and "how" you do it. It is much more about "who" does it and "why" you are doing what you do. There are certain characteristics that you must embrace in order to become a successful entrepreneur. The greatest asset of the entrepreneur is his mind and the focus of this book is developing and unleashing that invaluable asset.

"What lies behind us and what lies ahead of us are tiny matters compared to what lives within us."
- Henry David Thoreau

Kenneth Ogbebor

PART ONE

WHY?

Chapter One

YOU ARE FIRED!

"You are fired!"

Donald Trump (The Apprentice)

For most people, these three words "You Are Fired" are the most dreaded in their lives. For others these words are the stuff nightmares are made of. They wake up early, stay at the office late, take work home, fast, pray, play dirty, kiss butts, kick ass..., do just about every and anything not to hear these three words. I have got some breaking news and some bad news for you; **somebody is going to get fired!** Somebody has to be fired! Somebody ought to be fired! Some people get fired first day on the job while others, wait for thirty five years before they get fired. From casual workers, to entry level employees, to senior managers, directors and even CEOs, we are all potential targets for the work place snipers out there.

A job is only temporary. You can never know what might happen to your job. In the 1950s, 60s and 70s, jobs were more stable and you could have a job that would last as long as 10, 20 years, or even 50 years. Today however, it is much more different because of the metamorphosing dynamics of the global economy. Cross border trading of commodities and services and the flow of capital and rapid spread of technology has led to the continual integration of market frontiers. The world is so interconnected that international boundaries barely exist anymore when it comes to trade and economies and even competition in the job market. Just the way businesses are competing for clients in a global space, you are competing for jobs with the entire world.

Some in previous generations lost their jobs to mechanized farming and piled into factories. They set up unions to avert such inevitable job loss. Then the factories shut down and the search for job security continued. What difference does it make? Sooner or later, somebody is going to get fired. If the computer and computer aided manufacturing have not taken your job, or your job has not been outsourced to a place with lower wages, still watch your back. A kid may be writing a scrap of codes that will become an app that might just send you packing.

In this era of downsizing, rightsizing, computerization, optimization, outsourcing, multitasking, multiple jobs, freelancing, cost cutting, global economic meltdown, globalization, financial upheavals, unprecedented competition...somebody is bound to get fired, but nobody said it has to be you.

Some bosses get a kick from squeezing the trigger and "firing" people. When they talk about someone being "trigger happy", it usually refers to the person with the gun. Nobody will be happy to look down the barrel of a gun, and to know that a bang he may not even get to hear, can severe him from all existence. What if you are the one doing the firing instead of being the one used for target practice?

Someone said that employees do just enough not to get fired and employers pay just enough to keep you on the job. I find it hard to fathom why someone will invest the most productive part of his life under a dark ominous cloud doing just enough not to get fired. For some people, their sense of identity and self-worth is tied to their job. So being fired from the job is like losing their life's essence. And there have been many cases of people taking their lives or getting into serious depression or other serious emotional distress, because they lost their job.

Cheer up peeps, I have got some bad news, somebody is going to get fired. This is not "The Apprentice" and you are not Donald Trump. The news is not meant to kill you, but to make you stronger and like I said earlier, it will be more fun if you are the one pulling the trigger.

Like most kids from my generation, I grew up with a steady stream of movies from the American Midwest or what was rather called the "wild, wide west". I remember in these movies, gun duels often took place inside the bars, on the streets, or in front of court houses and those street duels went down most times in the full glare of everyone around. Two men stand facing each other, each with a gun in their holster. You may hear a shot or two depending on how fast both men are. As the echo of the shots rings out in the distant hill, there will be one man left standing. For me, the job place is a similar scenario with the goal for you and me to be the last man standing after the smoke clears.

No one goes for a cowboy gun duel without a gun in his holster. And it would be suicidal to stand out there in the street with an unloaded gun. It is like a sitting duck just waiting for its head to be plucked off. Yet most people are at jobs where their boss has the sword of Damocles continuously hanging over their heads. And they do not even have a pen knife in response. What kind of work place do you think we would have if everyone had their gun holstered, fully loaded and ready to go? Simply, the rules of the work place will change dramatically. This book is about turning the tables on your boss. This book is about having a ready response for the work place bully we call "boss".

What is the difference between a "termination letter" and a "resignation letter"? They are basically the same thing. Both are severance letters. One is the bully firing his staff and the other is the staff saying to the bully, this far and no further. Bosses never want to get to a place where they hire a staff they cannot fire. So why should you stay in a place where you cannot fire your boss? You might become a perpetual slave for the organisation. I advise that you have your resignation letter ready, it may be your last trump card, but do have it ready. I have seen many cases where people are fired and they gather the entire work force, their community, family, cats and dogs to join in begging to get their jobs back. I have also seen people drop their resignation letter and the chairman of the board invites them for a private chat in the lavishly furnished and luxurious pent house suite and starts making mouth-watering offers, so that his staff would not fire him. I tell you both letters are basically the same, the only difference is who is doing the firing, and by God, it had better be you.

This may not be the west, but it is still akin to a wild terrain. And whether we agree or not, somebody is going to get fired. The die is cast, the stage is set, there is anticipation in the air, no one will go back for a drink without blood soaking the dust on the streets; but why must it be your blood. Why don't you reach in your hip pocket and let your trigger happy boss feel the silver bullet and for a change, let the boss bite the dust and his blood be restitution for the many careers, hopes, dreams and aspirations, he has cut short in their prime. Do not get me wrong, the boss is not a bad guy, he is just doing his job, playing by the rules like the County Sherriff in those western movies. It is sometimes a case of fire or be fired.

My goal here is not to tell you why people get fired and help you not to get fired. People get fired for any and every reason, and some even get fired for no reason. Struggling not to get fired is like postponing the inevitable. It is better to be prepared to be fired and take it to the next level of firing your boss. Whether you are a rookie or a veteran, good at the job or a slouch, friend of the boss or foe, the very nature of jobs and the volatility of our present economic environment can never guarantee the job security that was partly enjoyed by our predecessors.

It was Helen Downing who said "Ultimately, life is a temporary job. One you will eventually get fired from" So do not take your job and even your life too seriously. Les Brown said "Don't sweat the small stuff; because it's all small stuff". You are not getting out of life alive, so spend the time you have planning your exit. This much is true when you get a job. See every day you spend on the job, from the first, as one less day on the job. Ultimately the chickens come home to roost. You are going to exit someday, but the real problem is when you are not ready for it.

Getting fired is nature's way of telling you that you had the wrong job in the first place.

Hal Lancaster

Chapter Two

SECURITY THREAT

"Security is mostly a superstition. It does not exist in nature, nor do the children of men as a whole experience it. Avoiding danger is no safer in the long run than outright exposure. Life is either a daring adventure, or nothing."

Helen Keller

In the twenty first century, the word security has acquired monumental popularity. The world has moved rapidly from the times when wars were fought with sticks and stones within a small geographical location to times when security threats have gone multi-dimensional and the impact of a local threat can spread globally in a short time. The threats to individual, national, or global security is no longer localised but globalised. And any event in one part of the world quickly resonates in other parts of the globe with its effects felt all around the planet. Every world summit today must have global security on the agenda and yet the world does not feel any safer for those who seek security in it.

Some people develop a sentimental, emotional and of course a financial attachment to their jobs. To love your job is a great thing. I love what I do. But to fall in love with a person or a job that is not in love with you is a serious security threat and a recipe for disaster. Life itself should have taught us that it is an exercise in futility to sacrifice ones self for a job, whereas the job is self-serving, feeding off you as its sacrifice.

It is most pitiable when some people sacrifice true joys, friends, family, integrity, values, even their health in pursuit of the ever elusive job security. They think that by putting in more time, energy, expertise or other resources, they can secure their jobs for life, but this is not usually the case. Like I said earlier, no boss wants to "hire a person they cannot fire"; it is a cliché in human resource management. Some people try to make themselves indispensable to the system, but the bad news is; you are not. Wake up and read the hand writing at the bottom of the page, no matter what you think you are bringing to the table, no organisation wants staff that can hold them to ransom. One day you will show up, and the table will not be there, and you will be left to rue all the invaluable things you have lost and the irreparable damage you have done to yourself in pursuit of job security.

One of the basic instincts of man is the need for security. According to Maslow's hierarchy of needs, the need for security or safety comes second, just behind Physiological needs. Seeking security is thus not bad in itself, but the real issue is our understanding of security and more importantly the means employed to achieve this security. There has never been job security in any age or dispensation. In the agrarian age, farms failed, people were injured, lands were lost, there were natural disasters like floods, droughts and for just about any other reason, people still lost their jobs. This was also true in the industrial age and in our present age; seeking job security is still living a lie. Organisations are in a continuous vortex of evolution, economic policies change rapidly, technology is advancing at lightning speed, product life cycle is getting shorter by the day, and competition is no longer localized, but globalized. It is possible that the person competing with you for the same job lives on the other end of the globe, and they can deliver such jobs from the confines of their homes.

Most people know, and research has shown that people tend to produce better results under an atmosphere devoid of distractions such as the fear of losing one's job. "Just about nothing is worse than uncertainty, and the dread of being unemployed, and it can actually be worse than the reality of being laid off", said Tinne Vander Elst, a postdoctoral researcher in organizational and personnel psychology at the University of Leuven in Belgium.

"When people know they will lose their job, they deal with it and their well-being increases," she said. "The really difficult situation is when people are in an insecure position, because they feel powerless."

"Research indicates that job insecurity reduces both physical and mental health, increases burnout, reduces job satisfaction and decreases work performance," said Dr. Vander Elst. Although some have theorized that a little insecurity is not a bad thing because people might work harder to keep their jobs, she said studies showed that "any amount of job insecurity is not good".

How can people live one day, one week, one year, ten years or more always with this fear of losing their job?

Available data also reflects that most heart attacks happen on Monday morning. According to Dr. Stephen Sinatra, research has shown "an 'outpouring' of stress hormones, such as cortisol and adrenaline, occurs within working people on Mondays. These findings were substantiated in a study of 683 patients, predominantly middle-aged men with implanted defibrillators and a history of life-threatening ventricular arrhythmias. The data led researchers to conclude that Monday is the most stressful day of the week when it comes to risk factors for heart attack. He believes that "your body always remembers and anticipates stressful events" and that can trigger the stress hormones.

The first time I read this, I said to myself, how come people can be so scared that their heart actually packs up on them because of work? People who are actively pursuing their passion, will jump out of bed on Monday, Tuesday or Saturday and get busy to bring their dreams to fruition. But for those who are going through the ordeal called jobs every week, it seems Monday morning is the worst thing to happen to them and they are so glad when they say, "Thank God it's Friday.

According to businessdictionary.com, Job security is defined as the "assurance (or lack thereof) that an employee has about the continuity of gainful employment for his or her work life. Job security usually arises from the terms of the contract of employment, collective bargaining agreement, or labour legislation that prevents arbitrary termination, layoffs, and lockouts. It may also be affected by general economic conditions".

More than six in 10 workers in a recent Washington Post-Miller Center poll worry that they will lose their jobs to the economy, surpassing concerns in more than a dozen surveys dating to the 1970s. This increasing fear of job loss is also reported in many other economies. In each of the economies, the fear today is a lot higher than it was in previous generations. This fear of job loss is not restricted to the low income segment only. It cuts across every segment of the job market and this fear is serious enough that it leads to worry.

And the economic condition in our day has had nothing but adverse effects on job security. Simple things like web design to more complex things like design and manufacturing of electronics and computers, business consulting and even larger products and projects can be ordered, paid for, produced and shipped seamlessly from anywhere across the globe just at the click of the computer buttons. Talk about tremendous competition. In the light of these changing times, we should position ourselves not to be swept away or overwhelmed by the flood of change.

There have been people who lost their jobs, and felt a weight lifted off them. Even though they did not have a clear plan or promise of how the future would pan out, holding down the job was like a weight dragging them down.

True security can only be found in seeking financial security instead of job security. What is financial security and what will it take to be financially secure? People define financial security in various ways with all connoting a situation where you have so much money that you never have to worry about money.

For some people, it is having a certain amount of money in the bank. The problem with defining financial security in these terms is that having $10 million, $50 million or even $1 million is a pie-in-the-sky dream for most people. We would all like to have millions of dollars, and it is not bad to aspire to that goal. The problem is, if we define financial security by such large amounts of money, most of us will believe that it is out of our grasp. Instead, we should use a realistic definition of financial security that can be achieved whether somebody makes $10,000 a year or $1,000,000.

Financial security is not making or having a certain amount of money. There are many people who have made millions of dollars and are not financially secure. Stories about musicians, superstar athletes and multi-million-dollar lottery winners who end up in bankruptcy are so common that they have become a cliché. If someone makes $500,000 a year, but spends $600,000, are they financially secured? Of course not! I prefer a broader definition, one that puts financial security within the reach of anybody with a desire to improve their financial situation, a reasonable and steady income and a little bit of discipline.

Financial security also is not limited to being independently wealthy, having servants bring you martinis by the pool, and flying your private jet to exotic places to party with heiresses, super-models, and rock stars. If that is what you want, then go for it, but this is a very narrow definition of financial security.

Financial security consists of some basic things:

1) Being debt-free

Consider two people: Peter makes $35,000 a year. He has $250 in his savings account, and owes $10,000 on his credit cards. Sam makes $35,000 a year. He has $10,000 in his savings account, and owes $250 on his credit cards.

Which guy do you think feels financially secure? Which one sleeps better at night?

Certain debts are understandable, if the reason is justifiable, particularly in the long run, but the best thing is to stay out of debt. The real problem is that there are many people paying debts on things they had no business buying in the first place. When you owe somebody money, they have power over you. You go to work, even if you do not want to, because you have to pay back your debt. If you do not pay, you can be sued, your car can be repossessed, or your house can go into foreclosure. That doesn't sound like security to me.

2) Being in control of your expenses

As I mentioned earlier, if you earn $500,000 a year, but you're spending $600,000, you're on your way to the poorhouse. If you control your expenses so that they are less than your income, you can save and invest the extra money, and you are on your way to becoming financially secure. There are limits to which you can reduce your living wage, so you must strive to increase your earnings. And when your earning increases, do not allow your spending to grow as well, and sometimes even overtake your increased earnings.

3) Consistently increasing your savings/assets/net worth on a monthly basis

Most people have little to show for years or even decades of hard work. For whatever reason, they cannot or would not save money and they are one pay check away from being destitute. We should focus on saving money every month. It is a great feeling to watch your savings grow, especially because the interest compounds without any extra effort from you, but this basic interest on saving is often eroded by inflation. Instead of you working for money, your money can work for you. Money working for you is simply being knowledgeable enough about certain investments such that you can multiply your savings instead of seeing your savings eroded by inflation while it sits in a savings account.

4) Not being forced to work at a job you dislike just to pay the bills

Many people live pay check-to-pay check and are stuck at jobs they don't enjoy because they have to pay their bills. If they quit their jobs or were laid off, it wouldn't take long before they would be in dire financial trouble.

If you are debt-free, control your expenses, and focus on increasing your savings on a monthly basis, you can survive tough times, such as a layoff, for months, or even years, without a change in your lifestyle. You would also have the freedom to quit a job you do not like and take your time finding a new job, preferably one that you will enjoy or in the absence of one, you create your dream job.

5) Not having to worry about money

The greatest worry for too many people is money. Most of their decisions in life are predicated on or denominated by money. What will you do or attempt to do if you do not have to worry about money? Even creativity is stifled when people are constantly worrying about cash to pay bills and survive. Worry is the known root cause of many ailments and conditions. To be financially free is to be able to live life free of money worries.

Financial security is an admirable goal for which we should all strive. Even though there is no one size-fits-all definition, it is a worthwhile goal to pursue. However, it is important to define financial security so that it is achievable for the average person. Being debt-free, controlling our expenses, increasing our savings every month, doing what we love and not having to worry continually about money can lead to happy, fulfilling, and prosperous lives, and it is something that many people can relate to and see as achievable.

"I am in control of my own destiny now. There is no harder struggle and no bigger reward in the world of business than to be in it on your own!"

Scarlett Hill

Chapter Three

ARE YOU HAVING FUN YET?

"I never did a day's work in my life – it was all fun."–
Thomas Edison

If I say that the major goal of everyone is to have fun, some "very serious" people will take exception to the statement. But if I say that everyone wants to be happy, then more people would agree with me. No matter how it is said or how we define it, we all want to be happy, fulfilled, achieve our dreams, and reach our goals.

For some folks, this happiness is an ever-receding island. Like a goal that is elusive, exclusive and perpetually out of reach. The question I have for you is; if you are not happy today, when will you be happy? Someday? When will that day come? What about today? Jim Rohn said that "Happiness is not something you postpone for the future; it is something you design for the present"

I cannot understand why some people will work at a job they hate, with co-workers they tolerate, for a boss they loathe, earn a pay they do not appreciate, serve customers they put up with... and they do this all the productive days of their lives. One reason that is always good enough to fire your boss is the fun of the job. It is a known fact that people do better at a job they like than at the one they have to endure. Some people live all their lives at dead and boring jobs. They take the frustration of the job home and, by that mess up their home life and of course their whole life just for of a lousy job. It is not worth it.

I once heard the Nigerian football legend, Austin "Jay Jay" Okocha say that he can play football for free. The reason for this is that he enjoys the game that much. You can see it in the passion and flair he brings into the game. You can actually tell by looking at his face that he enjoys what he is doing. The fun does not in any way reduce the earnings from the job. For Jay Jay, as well as so many others, they earned figures that most people only dream about in the course of their playing career and they are still earning now. This is also true of musicians, artists, engineers, bankers and doctors and it can be true about anyone.

The truth is that the compass that guides every man is inside him. If you reach within and find what you love to do, you love it so much that you can do it for free, then do it well, do it for many people and people will be willing to pay you for it.

Somewhere inside every man is a yearning for significance and meaningful contribution to humanity. And this is only possible when we maximize the unique potentials on the inside of us. When Ralph Waldo Emerson said, **"what lies before us and what lies behind us is small compared to what lies within us"** he was right. Yet for most people, their unique contribution is lost in the maze of day to day routine at dead and boring jobs. Some people bury their dreams long before they die.

I have often said; "If you do not enjoy what you are doing, do something else". For some people, their identity, sense of self-worth or confidence, their peace and their happiness is closely tied to the work they do. So they amount to nothing in their own eyes if they see their work as not being up to their personal standard or not fulfilling their passions.

Most jobs have their downsides or not so fun moments, but every job should also have some fun moments, or exciting moments, or challenging moments or some aspect that makes you think, "I'm looking forward to doing that". If your job is all in the color grey, then it is not worth it. Life is too short to spend it only looking forward to quitting time. Friday should not be your best day of the week. Everyday can be a great day.

DO WHAT YOU LOVE OR LOVE WHAT YOU DO

For some folks, finding what they love and being able to do it comes almost naturally to them. Yet for others, the lines traced by their passions and career paths seem like parallel lines that will never intersect. So if we say, do what you love, what happens when the cards life deals you do not present you with opportunities to do what you love? At least, at the present moment in time, do you sit by and do nothing?

The advice "do what you love" follow your childhood passions, and live happily ever after is really intended for people who have found what they are passionate about and they have an opportunity to take up that passion profitably. It may not be financially rewarding right now or ever but the fulfilment will suffice for people who are really living their dreams. For others, before they can do what they love, they have to do many things first. So that they can come to a place where they can do what they love. Balance is the key to life and that is why creating a balance of "loving what you do" and "doing what you love" must be established.

You may be passionate about basketball, but the chances of you making it to the NBA are very slim, necessary natural endowment is a must, luck or opportunities will play a part before we talk of other things like discipline and passion to pursue the dream. Yet you can still get involved in the NBA by owning an NBA team. Yeah! You bet that will be something to own an NBA team or a football team depending on your passion. The deal is that you might have to go make your money in the oil and gas, real estate, banking or any other traditional sector to be able to acquire the club and thrust yourself into your dream passion. You can as well be involved in many ancillary fields to the area of your passion. You can coach, be a commentator, a reporter, or any of the other back room staff that are invaluable to the success of the whole enterprise.

Similarly, you may love traveling, but no one is going to pay you a dime for discovering the Great Wall of China or the Eiffel Tower. Yet, some people have created travel magazine, television programs or even blogs about travelling that have earned them as well as anyone in many other traditional fields. Some people follow a dead end passion because they have developed a sentimental attachment to whatever is their dream with no innovation or inventiveness in their approach.

Now this is not to discourage you from following your passions to become a doctor or a lawyer or an insect photographer for endangered species for that matter. But it is to let you understand that to become a good photographer for example, you need the right gears, training, network and funding to enable you practice your passion at an excellent level. So if you have to teach history lessons to set yourself up properly, by all means do it. That will just be a stop on your road to somewhere, not a destination. If you wander off with your Kodak camera and rolls of films, you will end up a frustrated, mediocre, amateur photographer for life.

For some folks, music may be their passion, but what kind of music will they make if they cannot afford training or even studio time to record their tracks or good music videos to promote their songs. At a higher level, they will be badly served if all they know is music with no understanding of music business. So an education, a career in a different field, or an adequate source of income, even if in the interim will do them a world of good in helping them launch and advance their music career.

There is a difference between following a dead-end passion and following the passions that will bring success in your life. The greatest challenge with taking the advice "do what you love " without the balance of "loving what you do" is that "doing what you love" is often unrealistic, not in demand and comprised of decisions made with emotions. So as the bible says, "Whatever turns up, grab it and do it. And heartily! This is your last and only chance at it..."(Eccl 9:10-The Message). Even if you are not doing your ultimate dream job, loving what you do is the only way you can do it well enough to be exceptional, and develop the expertise that will put you in high demand. And the skills that you learn on this present employ will be invaluable when you get to your ultimate deployment. This is why a great workplace advice I give often says "Do not just work for what you earn, but also what you learn"

It is important to be paid to follow your passion; it allows you to sustain your message. Even if you are doing what you love, it will take you a couple of years to gain recognition and mastery in your industry. Without a doubt, unexpected obstacles will come your way, and sometimes pure passion is not enough to sustain you. Earning enough from what you do allows you to master your passion and develop clients. It also gives you room to make mistakes and learn as you grow. These mistakes include following the wrong passion, and you must be willing to change direction should you find yourself in a dead end place because of a childhood dream or passion.

Doing what you love will allow you to sustain your path. If you are truly passionate about it, then you will be spending many hours a day crafting, experimenting, and improving the skills that will eventually make you a master at it. Loving what you do can create the same effect even though you know you are only in it for the time being. If you do not love what you do, it becomes drudgery and boredom for you and others. You will never get better at a job you loathe. If you look at your long term dream, you can bear this passing phase with a straight face, love it till you leave it.

So if you are yet to find what you love doing, fall in love with what you have found to do. Have fun, what else is there?

"Choose a job you love, and you will never have to work a day in your life."

- Confucius

Chapter Four

EASY DOES IT?

"If you would only recognize that life is hard, things would be so much easier for you."
— *Louis D. Brandeis*

A famous quote says; "If you like things easy, your life will be hard, if you like things hard, your life will be easy". Very often, I have heard people complain that "life is hard" and my first question is "compared to what?" Simply put, this is life, take it and live it.

There are so many people who have all the dreams, visions and illusions of grandeur, yet they never dare to step out of the boat. Some are so scared that they do not even get off the shore and step on the boat. They wait by the shore line and watch people sailing by. Some have been immobilized by a few tales of mishap down the river of life and they have vowed not to venture into the stream of things. Some have had some bad experiences and have said "never again". Others just float on the river and go wherever the waves carry them.

The greatest challenge of going with the flow is that you seldom arrive where you intended. There is no greater joy, than to accept the challenge of life, grit your teeth if you have to and face it head on. If it is hard, then play it hard. Learn the rules of engagement, do not play foul of the rules, stay in line, and do not flunk the test.

This is simply life, what else could we call it. The rewards of life are for those who pass the test life puts in their way. It is a natural sifting mechanism that discriminates against the faint hearted.

One comfort in the difficulties of life is that, "life is not fair, it is even". It is not the hand that life deals you that matters; it is how you play the hand. If success were easy, every failure would succeed. The challenges are what separate the winners from losers, contenders from pretenders, and champions from the minnows.

Everyone gets their fair share of the winds of life. What use is good wind if neither you, nor your boat, nor your sail is prepared? According to Whitney Young Jr., "It's better to be prepared for an opportunity and not have one than to have an opportunity and not be prepared". If you are so scared of the difficulty of rowing, and as such do not set out on the journey to financial freedom, even if a good wind comes your way, you would not know, because you are not where the action is. Even if you win a jack pot or get an unexpected windfall, it will not leave you any better. Your output is only consistently as good as your internal mind-set and skill set.

There is no free lunch. The Chinese proverb says, "There is nothing as expensive as something gotten for free". On the journey of success, the true value of the process is not in the end result only, but very much in what you become in the process. You develop yourself in the dark days when life's challenges seem to overwhelm you. You develop resilience, resourcefulness, tenacity, redefine your goals, refocus your energy, develop your values. You get to know yourself better and of course know life better.

Adversity has advantages. Life was not meant to be easy. Success is discriminatory. It is only reserved for those who are willing to face the challenges, hold on against the harsh weathers and rise to the summit. Some of the successful people around us are not who they are because they had an easy ride in life. Some of them had to go through adversities and challenges. They are who they are because of and in spite of the adversities they had to overcome. Success without challenges is triumph without glory.

Those who succeed have not had an easier deal in life. Their lives were more or less as hard as every other person's life. They could have given up or given in just like some other people. Not every successful person today was born with a silver spoon. When you hear their stories, most of them came from obscure and humble backgrounds. It actually makes a better read, for the successes of today to tell their "rag to riches", "grass to grace" and "gory to glory" stories. Too many people are carried away by where people stand today and do not hear or take notice of the process that brought them where they are. The hard work that they had to put in to become who they are is very often the difference between them and others.

An African proverb says, "When the poor are told what it will take to become rich, some would rather be poor". This is similarly true of many people. There are too many people who will not pursue their dreams because of the hard work required. Talent may be given to all, but skill can only be honed on the anvil of hard work. There is so much fun in the process. It is not too hard, it is just life. My friend Theo once had a T-shirt that had this inspiring inscription "Life Is Tough, PLAY HARD"

Some people desire the finer things of life, but they are often held back by the requirements to bring their desires to fruition. They only want to take the easy road. So they are stuck in their comfort zone. Someone said that "life begins at the end of your comfort zone". If you never reach beyond your present grasp, you will remain where you are. It is in stretching to reach what is beyond our present grasp that we grow and become better. We must learn to let go of whatever makes us average. John Maxwell wrote a book titled "The Enemy Called Average". Sincerely, average is a failing formula. The world does not reward mediocrity. And excellence cannot be achieved on the bed of ease. Easy does it? I don't think so!

It is easy to stay at a job you hate because you are afraid of the hard work or uncertainty of stepping out on your own and thus never know what you could have achieved. It is easy to continue to do the same old thing that does not work, instead of reaching for the new with uncertain outcome and requiring you to change and stretch. It is easy to blame other people or the government for your lot in life instead of taking responsibility for yourself. It is easier to criticize than be part of the people who solve societal problems and many earn so much in the process. It is easy to live off other people like your parents or siblings or the government instead of getting in the game and taking the rough and tumble of earning your own bulks. Easy does it? I don't think so!

Success is reserved for those who are not afraid to take life head on. For those who can look life in the face and like Simba, can say "I walk on the wild side, I laugh in the face of danger" or like Miles O'Keefe, they know that for some things in life "The hard way, the only way". It is the exclusive preserve of those who are willing to do "Whatever it takes" to get to the winners circle. Easy does it? I don't think so!

It is easier to give up when you face hard times, forgetting Robert Schuler's timeless advice that "Tough times never last, but tough people do." It is easier to turn-tail and run when we fail forgetting that success is moving from failure to failure without losing enthusiasm (Winston Churchill). Easy does it? I don't think so!

It is easier to quit when we make mistakes forgetting that even the genius Einstein said "He who has never made a mistake, has never tried anything new". It is easier to dodge challenges, yet hope to win in life, because we forget that "challenges are the breakfast of champions". It is easier to makes excuses for where you are because you do not realise that "he that is good for making excuses, is seldom good for anything else" (Benjamin Franklin). Easy does it? I don't think so!

It is easier to try to avoid the long and lonely roads and the uphill climbs on the way to success and try to shunt process, because we forget that "there is no shortcut to a place worth going" and "Those at the top of the mountain didn't fall there." (Marcus

Washling). It is easier to sit on the divan of the idle and bemoan the lack of opportunities instead of realising that "Good things come to those who hustle while they wait" and that they have missed many opportunities because they were "dressed in overalls and they looked like work" and that "It is better to be prepared for an opportunity and not have one, than to have an opportunity and not be prepared" (Whitney Young Jr.)

Easy does it? I sure don't think so!

"It is not because things are difficult that we do not dare, it is because we do not dare that they are difficult."
- Seneca

Chapter Five

RAISE THE ROOF

Entrepreneurial profit is the expression of the value of what the entrepreneur contributes to the production process.

-Joseph Schumpeter

I have heard the phrase "raise the roof" used many times very often in music circles. I think it is about time everybody throws their hands in the air and raise the roof on their earnings. One of the most amazing things I know about the business environment is that there is no limit to profit. Say what! You heard me right. There is no limit to profit. How come some people's incomes are fixed and predetermined? It is because they are earning a salary and not earning profit.

I once heard a story about a factory that had a problem with one of their machines. All the maintenance personnel around had done all they knew to do to put the machine back in order but with no success. After all their efforts had failed, they invited someone to assess the machine and help them put it back online. The man showed up, did an extensive check, after which he told them to tap a certain part of the machine with a hammer. They were all happy to see the machine came back to life. A few weeks later, they got an invoice from the man with a bill of one million dollars. The company executives queried the man, arguing that all he did was just to tap a part of the machine. They required he send a breakdown of his bill. He sent them a breakdown as follows: *Tapping the machine, one dollar; knowing where to tap, nine hundred and ninety nine thousand dollars.* I am sure you get the moral of the story.

I have heard employees complain endlessly about what they earn to no meaningful end. Their complaints are most often directed at their bosses, employers, management or governments. What if I burst your bubble by saying, you are the one who determines what you earn. Some would argue with the above, but it is absolutely true. You may have begged to apply, or humbly applied for the job, but after all the formalities; you signed an acceptance letter that said you will abide by the condition of service, and of course accept the salary on offer. So who determined your wage, you or your employer? Think again! You could have shredded that sheet of paper into a million bits, but you put pen on paper and now you want to tell me your pay was thrust on you? I do not buy that. They made you an offer and you accepted and that made it a valid contract as prescribed by law. If the offering was not acceptable to you, you could have turned down the offer or made a counter offer. You may have taken the job for any or every of the reasons under heaven. It makes no difference, this is where we are, and your salary is your call. If you want more, ask for more. Not of your boss, but of yourself.

What are you bringing to the table? Some people do not matter to their organisation; they are just matter; have weight and occupy space. People get a salary commensurate with the value the employer places on their contribution to the organisation. There are people who make an organisation better just by leaving it. People get bonuses, raises, promotions and other incentives based on their contribution to the company bottom line. If you do not upgrade your skill, why should your pay grade change? New skills may not necessarily guarantee a pay raise, but without it, you may as well forget about increased pay in this competitive work place.

Salaries obviously do increase, but it is like salaries travel at snail speed while inflation is turbo-charged and living expenses is rocket propelled. So no matter how much you clamour for salary increase, it will have to overtake inflation and your consumption, to catch up with your aspirations. But profits can rise as fast as your exertion. If you put in more, you can get more. This is not the case with salary. The relationship between your input and what you get out of it is influenced by too many variables outside your sphere of control. When you are in charge of the ship of your financial destiny, you can trace a correlation between your effort and the results you are getting. If your endeavour gets good wind, you can be ashore without further rowing.

Case in point: Someone opens a business and starts to sell a couple of items or render some service. Let's say their turnover is a thousand dollars monthly. And profit after overhead cost is pegged at ten per cent of turnover, which implies a profit of a hundred dollars monthly. Assuming he gets a loan with favourable interest rate to increase stock, or gets suppliers credit from his supplier or gets a major order with advance payment and better margins, what will happen to his profit? His profit can literally shoot through the roof overnight and become a thousand dollars or more. There are many businesses that get this kind of growth in profits, but they do not increase the wage of their employees accordingly. The simple reason is that the business person is earning a profit and the employees are earning a salary.

Another case in point is in the real estate business. There are countless tales of people whose financial fortune has literally been turned around overnight because of one good deal. Most of them did not have to invest any substantial sum of money or perform a herculean task to earn their fee. For some, it was as simple as getting a buyer and connecting them with the seller and they could smile to the bank with a hefty commission. The receptionist, secretary or other employees do not directly benefit from this windfall except they own shares in the establishment or the boss is uncharacteristically magnanimous.

One of the greatest investments a man can make in life is to work once and earn endlessly from his work. People with a salary mentality will not get this at all. To them, it seems too good to be true on this side of eternity. For some, they even have to suffer a deduction for days they were absent from work, not to talk of trying to earn January and February salary for work you did in December. "No work, no pay" is not just a government mantra during industrial disputes; it is the day to day reality of work environments.

Have you ever heard of the words: royalties, retainer, maintenance agreement, franchising, mobilisation, licensing fee, renewals, rental fee and the likes? If these words are not in your regular vocabulary and present realities in your life, you may be working for only a single shot at glory, a single lame shot for a pot of lead instead of multiple shots for pots of gold. For some people this is bimonthly and for others, monthly. What they will receive for all the work done in the chosen interval is one pay check at the end of that interval. Whatever the interval, it is the ratio of input against the output that is the problem, or rather the ratio of work against the returns that matters.

The work life of some is like a rat race that even if they win, they are still rats. The deck is stacked against them and they are scurrying all over the maze trying to find their cheese not realising that there is a way out of the tunnel. Some people have to work for up to twenty four days a month, for about eight hours every day and sometimes even on weekends and at times at night. After this gruesome schedule, he gets a "handsome" reward, called a salary, a once for all pay check, that terminates the transaction of the last month and the rat race has to start all over again if he is going to be assured of a pay check at the end of the new month. Most people start from here, but those who understand the system quickly work their way out of this maze. Those who do not understand, stay here for ever. They talk about climbing the corporate ladder, not knowing that the ladder is leaning on nothing.

I am not ignorant of pension benefits and a gold watch after thirty five years of "meritorious service". Even if your pension bubble does not burst before you retire, inflation would have greatly eroded the value of your retirement saving. In actual sense, your pension savings is a deduction from your earnings. It is like deferring receiving due payment till later. As an incentive, your employer made their contribution and got a government licensed agent to manage the funds with a promise of bountiful yield when you retire. There are many people who have seen their retirement savings wiped out completely or substantially either by inflation, economic downturn or poor investment decision or mismanagement by their fund administrators. What use is a "gold watch" at seventy years when you could have been wearing one for many years prior? If you strike gold early, you give yourself a better chance of enjoying the reward of your labour for much longer.

I am not trying to paint a gory picture here, but when I look around me, I see that this is the experience of many of the people around me. Many of the same people will take offence at this representation and that is the more reason I am writing about this. Some people have their heads buried in the rat race and would not bother to lift their head to even look around them and really understand how this system works. This is the case clearly portrayed in the book "Who Moved My Cheese?" by Ken Blanchard.

How many billionaires have you seen who earn a salary? I know you can point to so many, but how many have you seen who earn a salary from someone else? Billionaires run their own companies. Not only do they fix their wages and pay themselves, their wages are just a token, they do not live off it. They own the orchard. The true scenario is that the company can pay for everything from their house, to their cars, vacations, groceries and just about anything. The beauty of this system is that they are sheltered from paying heavy taxes both as a company on their profit and as individuals on their income. This is called "tax avoidance" or "tax reduction", which is completely legal as against tax evasion which is illegal. They earn, spend, and the remainder is taxed. Whereas employees earn, then they are taxed and they spend the rest. It is about how you understand the system, and by what set of rules you play.

There are a lot of people who work very hard in the system, but they have no inkling how the system works. This reminds me of one of the phrases from a movie I had seen, "We run things, things don't run we". For these people, they have become pawns in a system that is tipped against them right from the start, in spite of the entire facade that their employers place before them.

Have you ever heard employees talking about return on investment (ROI)? Not at all, instead they talk about wages, salaries, allowances, raises, bonuses and the likes. The fact that the language of the employee and the employer are different is a clear indication that they are playing in different leagues. The rules are different and the returns, you sure bet they are radically different. You cannot get a lions return if you go hunting with fleas. Both returns may be bloody, but only one will have flesh and bones and be big enough to feed a pride.

At the other end of the spectrum, it is a whole different ball game. You can work once and earn for the rest of your life and even the generations yet unborn can keep earning from the work done. A simple case in point is software development. You can develop a software or in our present day an App (application). For immediate returns, you can sell to the highest bidder and cash in on your invention. Some developers will license this software or App to end users who in turn pay certain fees to the developer. These fees might seem small, but when earned from many users the world over and compounded over a long period of time, they can become a steady stream of income that runs into multi millions and make the owners not just rich today, but also tomorrow.

Another ready example is the author or the musician. Even though writing a book is not a very lucrative venture in itself, when an author writes a book, he can start to earn from selling copies of the book. It is simple arithmetic to know that the more the copies he sells, the more he will make even though he wrote the book once. So a bestselling author will make money from selling millions of copies of a single book that he wrote. That is not all there is to it. He can license reprints of the same book in various places and receive a licensing fee. No need to worry about printing and distribution; he just grants the licence and pockets his money. If the book is translated to other languages, he will make more money, with no further work done. If the book is adapted for a movie, the author does not have to worry about the script, the set, recording, financing the movie or its distribution, once the license has been granted for the adaptation of the book to a movie, or television series or documentary, the author can smile to the bank. So you can write one good book and smile to the bank, again and again and again. That is what we call "Cash Flow".

This much is true of real estate developers or owners of rental properties who invest for cash flow. This is also true for artists, caterers and many other professions. It is not about the profession, all that matters is how you play the game of work. If you shoot for the long term multiple returns for every work done, you can work once and earn again and again.

A good caterer can come up with a unique recipe and bake a very delicious cake. She will make money from baking more of that cake and selling them. If all she knows is how to bake, she will continue to bake cakes to earn a living until she becomes baked by her excessive exposure to the oven heat and become strained by her continuous exertion at the kneading trough. But if she understands the business of baking, she can patent her recipe, employ and train others to expand the production and distribution of the cakes. This will increase cash flow and if done right, she can come to a stage where the business can run with reduced personal input. She can further license her recipe to others and receive royalties. She can expand and create a franchise out of the cake business, still more money in the bank. What if she does a cook book, opens a catering academy, produces training materials and DVDs? That's real cool money. So which would you rather be? A very good baker who only knows how to bake or a good baker who knows the business of baking?

The difference is subtle, but one thinking will create a job and the other will create a cash flow with endless possibilities. The difference is not obvious to very many people, but for those who know, they can raise the roof on their earnings. This is radically different from the thinking that someone else is the determinant of your earning, when you can create multiple streams of income.

Creating multiple streams of income is not about working "twenty five hours a day, eight days a week". It may seem that rich people work long hours, but the difference is that they do so on their own terms. It is about creating passive income that will keep spinning money like a money machine without you having to work it 24/7. It is often a onetime work or investment with very little continuous input, which in some cases is as simple as cashing in ripe investments.

Diversifying your income stream is crucial to protecting yourself and your family against the unavoidable ups and downs of global economic and industry cycles. Because of the financial risks that come from relying on one source of income, such as a job or a business, consider creating at least one or more additional streams to generate cash flow.

Your additional income streams can be active, passive or a combination of the two. Active income or passive income refers to the amount of time and attention required to generate the income stream. You can convert your hobbies or other talents or skill to additional sources of income. People have been known to have resigned their jobs because what they started as an additional stream of income has grown or has the capability to grow into a substantial revenue source. You can turn your interest, hobby, passion, talent or skill into income streams if you do not have the money to go into real estate, financial market or other capital intensive business ventures.

In order to build true wealth, you must be able to live within your means. In a case where it is impossible to cut your spending any further, or you just do not want to sacrifice anymore, it is imperative that you create a new source of income. There are only two ways to live within your means, either spend less or make more money. Making more money is definitely a better option considering also that the cost of living in many economies is getting higher by the day.

You may keep your job, but for anyone who values financial security and ultimately desires financial freedom, creating at least one additional stream of income is no longer a luxury. It has become a necessity. This truly is one of the not-so-obvious secrets of how the wealthy become and stay wealthy, which unfortunately is not taught to the masses.

"Poverty is first a mentality, then a reality".
Kenneth Ogbebor

Chapter Six

WHO WANTS TO BE A MILLIONAIRE?

If you want to be a millionaire, think like a millionaire
Bassey (TV Drama, Bassey & Company)

Life is not a game show. Some say life is a game, but not everyone is taking it as child's play. Some are real serious about this game while others are on the side lines looking in. Inflation may be inexorably eroding the value of your local currency, but achieving millionaire or billionaire status (depending on the value of your currency) is still an impressive and motivating goal. More importantly, it is an eminently attainable goal with hard work and careful planning and dutiful execution. There are more self-made and first generation millionaires in our generation than any other time in history. An African proverb says, "There are many roads that lead to the market" Though there are no hard and fast rules to becoming a millionaire or a one size fits all approach, there are some pathways that are more likely to take you to the millionaires club instead of becoming one of those who fall by the way side.

When thinking about how to accumulate say, a million dollars or more, there are some key issues that we must consider. First, a job must be available and accessible for it to offer a high likelihood of thrusting someone into the millionaire status. For instance, playing in a professional sports league dramatically increases the odds of earning enough to become a millionaire, but professional sports employ only a tiny fragment of the entire population. Likewise, virtually every Fortune 500 CEO gets a million-dollar pay package (or better), but there are only 500 of those jobs available and the entry requirements are utopian at best.

What's worse, while I do understand the importance of hard work for athletes, there is an element of natural talent that must be present for this to be an option. No amount of hard work can make eagles of turkeys. Hard work draws on your natural endowments. Likewise, while being an A-list movie star or musician certainly pays well, it too relies on an all-too-rare combination of talent and luck. Accessibility can also refer to the training required and the number of opportunities that exist in a given field. There are some professions that can indeed pay quite well at the upper echelons, but that often requires a degree from one of a very limited list of PhD programs. Likewise, while there are academic disciplines that can pay surprisingly well (astronomy, for instance), relatively few jobs come available in a given year. Clearly, a job must pay well if one is to build a seven-figure net worth from it. It is not all about salary, though. It is also important for a career to have the duration necessary to build the requisite amount of wealth.

There is an old cliché that parents want their kids to be and/or marry doctors, lawyers or engineers. It may be clichéd, but there is an element of truth and logic to it. For example, physicians, surgeons, lawyers, engineers, architects, and many other professions do in fact boast median pay of over $75,000 a year in most countries.

It's not quite that simple, though. While all of these professions can look to long careers (and pay usually increases with experience), there are sizable entry demands, including multiple years of expensive post-graduate schooling. It's also worth noting that median pay does not mean a guarantee - while practicing law can indeed pay very well, many lawyers make much less than the median pay. Political scientists, economists and nuclear plant technicians may all potentially earn a lot, but there are not many positions available in a given year and there is not much job growth. On the other hand, demand for medical professionals and computer engineers continue to grow at above-average rates.

While readers may be hoping for a map to careers where the roads are paved with gold, these maps just do not exist. That is due in part to the fact that there are so many different ways to get ahead and build towards that target of $1 million. Consider the following: a person who makes $60,000 and saves 20% of it will get much further much faster than someone who earns $100,000 and saves only 5%. Likewise, prudent investing is crucial. Whether you are self-employed or an entrepreneur, it is not just about what you make, it is what you keep that counts and whether you can invest that savings profitably. Even a doctor who saves $15,000 a year free and clear will need to work for over 65 years to have $1 million without any gains on those savings. Consequently, developing the skills and the discipline to save and invest effectively is almost as important as developing the skills for a six-figure salary.

Looking at income tax and net wealth data, the largest percentage of millionaires attain their wealth by running businesses. A person can take multiple paths to become the CEO of a major company. CEOs have come from the ranks of engineers, marketing managers and financial analysts. Often the common denominator is an MBA degree from a top-flight MBA program - a path that demands not only a fair bit of upfront monetary investment, but also a superior academic and professional background. Yet the above does not exclude people with less sterling academic records. Even though no fortune 500 company will hire a college-drop out without prior experience as their CEO, you can create your own career path to becoming a CEO or a millionaire by running your own business.

Starting and running your own business not only lets you put yourself in charge (and pay yourself whatever your business will support), but you also benefit if/when your business grows in value over time. You don't have to be the next Bill Gates, Steve Jobs or Mark Zuckerberg; even a modest local business can support a healthy salary for many decades.

Of course, it's not that simple. While many of the wealthiest people can tie their wealth to running a business (either their own or someone else's), there are plenty of entrepreneurs who struggle to make it from month to month or go out of business within a year or two of starting.

While anybody can start a business, the success of that undertaking is going to depend on a number of factors such as the quality of your idea, your willingness to work hard at it, the conditions of the local market and some factors that depend on you and others that are beyond you.

While no one should choose a career solely based upon its earnings potential, it is still a valid consideration. At the same time, aspiring millionaires need to consider how difficult it is to train for a profession, how likely it is that they can get jobs in their chosen fields and whether they will enjoy the work enough to stay at their jobs for decades. When all of those factors intersect, and you are willing to save and invest carefully, there are dozens of careers that can lead to a net worth in the seven figures before retirement.

Having a million doesn't make you a millionaire; it's having a millionaire mind-set that makes you one.
Efe Opkosio.

Chapter Seven

RETIRE RICH, RETIRE YOUNG

"The trouble with the rat race is that even if you win, you are still a rat".

-Lily Tomlin

My favourite quote on governance is by Ronald Reagan during his first inaugural address as president of the United States. He said, "In this present crisis we face, government is not the solution to our problem, government is the problem." What a damning statement on governance from the CEO himself. So many people are living their lives with no thought for their future. They think their retirement is secure in the hands of the government. They expect the government to take care of them in their old age. Nothing could be further from the truth. Most people get their hearts broken, late on in life, when they get to retirement age and realize that their accrued benefits which they expected to take care of them at retirement are either not there or inadequate to take care of them.

The image of retirement most of us grew up with and some of us still have is that of a frail old person, sitting in a recliner and just waiting to call time on life on earth. Other images include that of people living in so called retirement homes or old people's homes. These people can barely carry their weight. Most of them do not have the energy to enjoy their life like they did when they were younger. They may have money, but no energy to enjoy the money. Retirement age is set around 65 or 70 years, depending on country or industry. But who says you cannot retire rich and retire young? What if you re-wrote your own life story by yourself? And being the author, you can write the script and call retirement whenever it pleases you.

The only real shot at retiring rich and retiring young is firing your boss. If your boss fires you, young or old, you are in deep trouble. But if you fire your boss right, you can retire young and have the energy to enjoy your retirement. To retire means to call time on working because you have to work, and enter a new lease of life where you work because you want to work, and of course, you do what you want to do, and like Confucius said, you would not have to work for the rest of your life.

The average worker earns about a reasonable sum annually. So over the course of one's working life, most people can earn over a million dollars. But like we said earlier, no one ever got wealthy on what they earn; people create wealth from what they accumulate. And you cannot retire except your accumulated wealth or passive cash flow is sufficient to meet your daily needs and that of your family. Leave enough over for your other concerns like charity and causes you care about or challenges that confront you, whether you work or not.

Even though several people earn over a million dollars in their working life, most people work till retirement while some, work beyond that because they cannot afford to retire. For others, they are flat broke in as short as three months should they lose their jobs or be in between jobs. The major reason some people who have earned substantial sums in their life time cannot retire young or even retire at all in extreme cases is very often a result of lack of planning. When you have a retirement plan and you work this plan, it will influence every sphere of your life, both earning and spending. For most people, every salary increase or income growth or unexpected windfall is an invitation to more expenditure. They increase their living wages until it meets and then goes over their new earning and no thanks to the credit card and easy access to credit, it is easy to live above your means. At the end of the month, they are as broke as when they did not have the raise or moved to a better job or earned a higher income.

Instant access to credit via credit cards has created a society of debtors where people are continuously encouraged to live above their means. Savings is not just a culture to be encouraged, it is a lifestyle to be planned and lived religiously. Pay yourself first is not an invitation to self-pampering. It means that from whatever you earn, you save first, and spend what is left instead of the reverse where people spend first and save what is left. For most people, they save nothing because after spending, nothing is left except some debts and unpaid bills. A simple way to plan your retirement using savings as a vehicle is to first calculate what your monthly living expenses are. Then as you save, you can tell how long you will survive on your savings and passive cash flow, assuming there is no additional income, and of course leaving some extra for any unforeseen expenses. When your passive income becomes higher than your living expenses, you can cease to work because you have to and only work on what you want, just because you want to. That is the best retirement package you can arrange for yourself.

This is the age of instant credit because of the credit card. A lifestyle of indebtedness is only a card away and so many people are "swiping" away their financial freedom leaving them unable to retire, because they are too steeped in debt. Credit card makes it very easy for people to do impulsive shopping. They buy things they cannot afford, do not need or did not plan to buy now, and end up paying much more in credit card debts. The best advice I have heard on credit card is simple, "cut up all the plastics". Hold one if you must just for emergencies. Do not pile up debt just because you have easy access to credit. It will indefinitely push forward your retirement age and in extreme cases, if you can manage to retire or are forced to retire because of age, you definitely cannot retire rich, and of course not young.

There are many parents who argue that "Education is the best legacy that you can leave for your children". Thus the desire to achieve academic qualification is driven into many young people. This leads to the acquisition of academic intelligence. This academic intelligence does not directly translate into financial intelligence. There is more of academic intelligence, and so much information around us all, but like the saying, "water, water everywhere, but not a drop to drink". There is so much information everywhere but people are dying every day because of the personal dearth of financial intelligence or disregard for financial principles. Some people do not understand anything about money. They may be engineers, medical doctors or professionals in various fields, but when it comes to the subject of money, they are neophytes. Financial intelligence is not the same thing as academic intelligence. Jim Rohn once said; "Formal education will make you a living. Self-education will make you a fortune".

Financial intelligence is an understanding first of, what money is and what it is not. Then we can proceed to learn how to make it or earn it, save it and manage it, invest it and multiply it, share it and enjoy it. Most people's relationship to money is based on myths that have been passed from generation to generation. Some work all their life for money, yet they have never taken the time to really understand what money is, yet somewhere at the back of their mind, they hope to stumble on money. No wonder when they do stumble on money, they live true to the adage, "A fool and his money are soon parted".

The money game is a lot like football. It involves offence and defence. You must be good on both fronts to win the game. Offence is earning the money, just like scoring goals, and defence is everything else you do after making the money such as saving, managing, multiplying, investing...just like not conceding goals. To win the game of football, you have to score more than you concede. To win the money game, you must absolutely earn more than you spend and find a way to multiply what you have left over so that you can retire rich, and retire young. Just like football, talent is not enough, skill and strategy is more critical, particularly in the big leagues.

To argue that money is not important is ludicrous. Yet to think that money is the most important thing is dangerous. Money is not an end that we seek; instead money is a means to certain ends. Some people equate money to cash, but this is limiting. In its purest form, money is leverage, a means to an end or anything you can leverage to achieve your desired end. If some people want a car for example, they can buy one, either fully paid or via financing options. On the other hand, there are people who are paid to use certain cars and many other products. They are paid heavily just to show they use the products which is a form of endorsement of the product. They may not have cash, but they are leveraging their success in other areas to achieve the same end. They will achieve an even better end than someone who had cash to purchase the same product.

There is good reason why "human resources" is called human resources or human capital. It is the fact that you can leverage it for money or as a medium of exchange to get whatever you want. Exchanging money for everything is a narrow understanding of the power of leverage. If you must pay money for everything, you may run out of money no matter how much you earn. Pay for only the things you cannot receive through leverage. This will leave your money free to invest in profitable ventures. Returns from these investments can become a secure source of retirement funds.

To retire rich and retire young, you must start young. Many parents do not teach their children anything about money. They may leave them a fortune, but nothing more. When children understand money at a very early age in life, they stand the chance of being able to work the process and retire rich and retire young. We should not allow every succeeding generation to make the same mistakes the previous generations have made. Let the sacrifices of the past engender an easier future for our children. They will face their own challenges, but they do not have to fail where we did, when they can learn from us.

I think the notion of retirement is just a dreadful, dreadful idea and I hope I never have to do that
Micheal Moritz

PART TWO

HOW?

Chapter Eight

THINK LIKE A CEO

"Good Thinking, Good Product"

-Daewoo group

At the end of his extensive search for proof of his existence, the French philosopher, Rene Descartes concluded; "I think, therefore I am". His conclusion was that the fact that he can hold thoughts in his mind, even if they were thoughts doubting his existence, proved his existence. If according to Rene Descartes, our thought, or ability to think, is the proof of our existence, then it can follow that the result of our existence will be a product of our thoughts.

Our mind-set, mentality, thinking, attitude, outlook or life philosophy creates a system that determines our outcomes in life. Externally, two factories may look alike. The raw materials may be the same, but the internal configuration of the factory creates its operational system, just like the operating system of the computer. The operating system and additives during the production process determine the end product of the factories in spite of similar starting inputs. Systems determine the end product of any process. Even if the raw materials are the same, or the external input same, the output will mirror the system.

If we want to win, we must change how we think. Success is a choice. Every true champion knows. The mental game is the key. It is the greatest power. Most people never truly tap that power; they do not even know it exists. They go around thinking the same old thoughts and doing the same old things day in day out.

Different types of thinking can create different systems that may not be compactible and thus cannot run seamlessly within the same body. When we hold conflicting thoughts within ourselves, it causes us to falter when we walk and stutter when we talk. Singleness of mind creates power. It leads to focus and nothing is as powerful as focused effort. The laser beam is simply focused light, yet it is so powerful that it can cut through metal. Without focus, we dissipate energy on areas where we should not and we end up not being able to give our best to the areas we should.

Earlier, I said that CEOs think return on investment (ROI) whereas employees think salary. Also, most see the salary like getting something for nothing. They often forget what they had to put in, in terms of time, expertise, finances, and other inputs to get the salary. When a CEO gets any income, he looks at what he had to invest to receive that income, and the difference between the two values is what is called his return on investment, (ROI) or in simple terms, profit.

CEOs think of net worth, whereas salary earners see their salary as a total package. Some forget they had to buy their car to take them to work, fuel it, fix it or pay for the ride to get them to work. They forget the extended investment of time and money in education and trainings in order to be qualified to get the job and to do the job well. So their salary is not a total package for their consumption, like they have come to speciously believe. Some people actually run at a loss from what they earn on the job they are working. No wonder many of them earn an income but "there is more month at the end of their money", simply put, they are broke at the end of the month, their account is in red.

They have not taken the time to check the financial implication, the capital outlay necessary to take them back and forth from work every day, buy clothes to look the part, join clubs to feel belonged, join associations to be elite, pay dues to be legit, all so that they can keep their job. At the end of the month, their salary may not be enough to meet these entire obligations and leave anything meaningful over.

You are what you think. You are a product of your thoughts. Employers think differently from employees. If you change the way you look at things, the things you look at will change. CEOs think financial security whereas employees think job security. CEOs know that the road to success is paved with failure, but employees are averse to such risk, they prefer to play it safe. Developing a successful mind-set and habits is a precursor to a successful life.

THE ENTERPRENEURAL MIND-SET

Being an entrepreneur is very different from being an employee, and there is definitely an entrepreneurial mind-set that you will need to develop in order to secure your success whether as an employee or a self-employed person or an employer. Entrepreneurs see the world differently, but what I am talking about goes far beyond that. It is not a question of what is going on around them; it is more a question of what is going on inside them. In order to be a successful entrepreneur, you have to unlearn some of the things you learned in school or what you learn on the job from most employees.

When people talk about entrepreneurs, most people describe them as someone who starts a business. They go on to describe their characteristics such as , "visionary", "leader", "optimist", "persistent", "risk taker", etc. It is easy to describe entrepreneurs in terms of their characteristics or their actions. These descriptions are partially correct, because these are all manifestations that we are all capable of if we have or develop the entrepreneurial mind-set.

We are all born with the innate ability to survive; and survival involves innovative thinking. Being entrepreneurial is essentially about thinking and doing something that we may not have done before, in order to achieve a desirable goal or outcome. It is about assessing a situation, designing alternatives, and choosing an existing way, a new way, or perhaps a combination of ways, that we hope will lead us to something better; however we happen to define "better" at that moment. If our definition of better changes with time or our goals change, we innovate ways to achieve the new goals.

Some people believe that entrepreneurs are born, like it passes through the genes. So when they see others in entrepreneurial endeavours, they count themselves out. We are selling ourselves short if we do not define ourselves as entrepreneurs or capable of becoming entrepreneurs. If we choose to accept that "entrepreneurs" are the "other" people who take a chance, we create a self-limiting belief. This self-limiting belief stops us from acquiring the characteristics and developing the mind-set necessary for entrepreneurship. I see mind-set and attitude as the real differentiator of talent in our world.

When we think innovatively and act on that innovation, we are entrepreneurs. The brain qualities that make a great leader as well as a successful entrepreneur can now be mapped—and therefore they can be recreated. The brain is like a muscle. It can be exercised and trained to achieve specific, desired outcomes.

When you think and act differently when challenges arise, your small act can be considered an act of entrepreneurship. This act is manifested as the choice you make to alter your life; to go through the pain of detaching yourself from what you usually do and attempt a new course of action; the pain of choosing to be resilient in the face of adversity; the gut wisdom of taking a risk because you know that you just cannot keep doing "more of the same." Maybe it is starting a company; maybe it is presenting a new idea to your boss; maybe it is choosing to pursue a degree; maybe it is physically moving to another location...the choices are endless and we face them throughout our lives.

Some entrepreneurship training courses are really mental exercises. They help you develop the kind of mental skills you need to think, innovate, make decisions, take action and lead effectively. Sounds simplistic; but entrepreneurship skills can be learned-provided you are willing to work at it hard enough. If you find an entrepreneur you admire, learn their style, actions and approaches, read books on the subject areas as necessary, and experiment, see what works for you and do more of the same. It is not rocket science but it will definitely take work. Most people are not willing to put in the work necessary to develop these skills, so they give up on what they could have achieved as entrepreneurs.

Academic research on the psychology of entrepreneurs has shown that there is no single psychological typology (set of characteristics) that suggests an entrepreneur's success is guaranteed. From my experience and observation, I would like to highlight the following characteristics out of the many shared by successful entrepreneurs.

Re-Invent the Wheel

In order to develop a truly entrepreneurial perspective, you must begin again. No matter how long you have been in business or how long a thing has been done one way, it is important that you take on the perspective that you are starting it anew today. You will sometimes have to question your own answers and confront age-old tradition and set ways of doing certain things. Understand that when you propose new, you will always meet with opposition from the old, but change is the only way to guarantee tomorrow. Do not be distracted by people who want to keep things the same or those who say, it cannot be done.

Is There A Cause?

Causes are important to entrepreneurs in this age. Causes add dimensionality to your business. Causes add meaning to your business, beyond simply making money. Money is not an end but a means to an end. Making money is not a cause in itself but a necessity. A necessity does not need to be stressed every day, but a cause must be. If you pursue a cause, you stand a chance to make a difference even if you do not make money. If you pursue money, you may make money, but that may be all you will make.

Tomorrow Matters

Deal with today with tomorrow in mind. An entrepreneur does not bury his head in the grass and forget to look at the field. Even though he makes decisions on immediate concerns, he always keeps the thought of the future firmly at the back of his mind. You cannot make long term decisions based on short term considerations only.

Perseverance

The ability to withstand repeated rejection and disappointment is an essential part of an entrepreneur's makeup. Successful entrepreneurs are able to draw lessons from rejection, as well as prevent it from damaging their self-esteem. Essentially, you must be able to deflect the rejection away from yourself and use it as a spur to fix flaws in your business ideas. They understand that failure is an event and not a person.

Flexibility

Entrepreneurship is a tough space to play in. Unexpected challenges and problems appear constantly. You must be flexible enough in your thinking to roll with the punches, solve problems as soon as they crop up, and recover quickly from setbacks. Do not stay fixated on what is not working. Even the things that seem to be working are constantly being reworked to make them better. Innovation is part of an entrepreneur's daily life.

High Internal Locus of Control

Successful entrepreneurs have faith in their ability to determine their own success. They see that their own actions, decisions, and responses are what will make or break them - not what the outside world throws at them. This means that you need to take responsibility for doing the things that need to be done. You must understand that you are not a victim of circumstance but a product of your decisions.

Learning and Iteration

When a problem occurs, a successful entrepreneur sees it as a learning opportunity. The lessons an entrepreneur takes from any given situation are then used in successive iterations of the entrepreneur's ideas to develop and refine them. According to Alvin

Toffler, "The illiterate of the 21st century will not be those who cannot read, but those who cannot learn, unlearn and relearn."

Curiosity

A wide-ranging curiosity about how the world works and where things tie together is extremely common among successful entrepreneurs. Always keep your mind active – this will strengthen your ability to see things from different angles and think laterally.

Optimism

Despite all the difficulties inherent in the entrepreneurial lifestyle, successful entrepreneurs maintain an optimistic view of life and the world. Being optimistic about a situation could mean the difference between seeing it as an unsolvable problem or an opportunity to be explored.

Choose Courage over Fear

To be successful, you have to have courage and to become courageous, you have to do courageous things. Much of being successful is about going beyond what you think you are capable of, venturing into the unknown. Whether you fail or succeed, you will learn and grow. Entrepreneurs share some fears with other people, the difference is that they are not immobilized by their fears. They know that if you do what you fear, the death of fear is certain.

Believe In Yourself

Attitude is a mental choice irrespective of external circumstances. A negative attitude decreases success and a positive attitude creates success. Without that belief in yourself, you will lack a path to success. Success is something that is created. It's not something that merely "happens." When you firmly believe in yourself, you can achieve virtually anything. It's within this belief that you will find the power to create the resilience and fortitude needed to keep going when things get tough.

Gratitude

When you see life and career in terms of the lack in what you have achieved, you cannot drive your business up the ladder of success. This negativity will impede your progress. You must look at all you have and realize how greatly blessed you are irrespective of what others have or how far you may be from certain goals. When you have this attitude of gratitude, you stop suffering and complaining about the small stuff. Complaints create negative energy around you and this can impede creative thinking.

Discerning

At every point in time, there will be many things clamouring for your limited time, resources and attention. Selectivity creates success. You must think deeply and intelligently about the bigger picture and what it is you need for each step along the way to continue articulating and executing your business goals. Mindfulness means being aware of all angles and staying sharply in touch with the present so that you do not have to clean up mistakes in the future.

Be discerning of group dynamics: which person is the best at what job, which customers or deals will take you the furthest and what it is that each moment is calling on you to do or change to be the most efficient.

This list is not exhaustive, but developing these mind-sets gives you a compass to navigate the ever-changing tides on the way to business and financial goals. These mind-sets allow openness and flexibility while also providing you precise direction.

MIND-SETS THAT CAN KILL YOUR BEST IDEAS

Sadly, there are a few other frames of mind that often doom your entrepreneurship or possibly brilliant ideas before they get off the ground. Steer clear of these mind-sets.

The Fear Mind-set

A lot of entrepreneurs have their subconscious asking, "What's the worst thing that could happen if..." There is a time for risk assessment. That time is not when you are innovating. Only when you can articulate the value of your idea, and when you want it enough to commit the energy to pursuing that idea should you indulge in worst-case scenario thinking. Fear is the tomb in which many dreams are buried.

The Attachment Mind-set

There are entrepreneurs who hear just one answer to the question and then stubbornly chase that single outcome, banging their heads against brick walls and their fists against locked doors while all around them, hundreds of other answers are clamouring for attention. They might succeed eventually, battered and bloodied (or they might surrender), but either way, they will have a story of how business is a battleground or you have to fight like a dragon for your dream.

The Excitement Mind-set

The entrepreneur in this mind-set has an idea that is so cool it defies description. It is so amazing, fantastic and unbelievable that it has to be pursued at all costs. Excitement is not enough to carry an idea from innovation to execution. That takes true passion, determination, strategic thinking and, most of all, articulation. If you cannot describe how your idea will change someone's life , then selling anyone else on the idea is going to be tough.

The Enlightened Sceptic Mind-set

This entrepreneur has probably been beaten up and beaten down for being too excited or has had too many ideas fall out because they were fuelled only by excitement. So now their mind-set says that ideas are a dime a dozen, but ideas that make money are one in several millions, so it is the better part of wisdom to withhold any and all emotion until you see that this idea really could be the one that survives. There is no excitement, desire or passion. Therefore, there is no energy, commitment or determination available for exploration or implementation.

The How Mind-set

This mind-set insists that you know how you are going to do it before you even articulate the value you would bring to the world by seeing it through. This entrepreneur builds walls out of, "You don't know how to do that," and, "How are you ever going to get the money?" and "How do you think you will get in front of the people who might buy it?" Like risk management, "how" is part of the strategic phase, not the innovation phase. Do not fall prey to the "hows" before you have completely explored the "whys" and "whats."

Reinventing the wheel really does count as innovation, if it is a better wheel. And no one wants to see an idea for a better wheel killed because you were in the wrong mind-set when you asked the right questions.

SELLLING AND NEGOTIATION

When you are working for someone, you leave the selling to those in the sales team. Except you are in the sales team, you can just stay in your department, meet your schedules and deadlines, turn in your reports on time and do what else is required of you and you can be sure of a pay check at the end of the month. When you are in business for yourself, your most important assignment is going to be sales. Great sales people say that anybody can sell anything to anybody anywhere. Selling is not just important; it is the life line of the company.

It makes no difference what product or service you have, if the people who want it do not know, it is equal to winking in the dark. And even if they know and do not buy, you will soon be out of business. As an entrepreneur, you must sell your idea to your investor, or venture capitalist, your partners and then if the business gets off to a start, you have to sell your idea and culture to your staff, products to customers and opportunities to investors and venture capitalists.

Selling is dreadful to some people because they have a wrong idea about sales or sales people. In the final analysis, everyone is a sales man. You are either selling a product, a service or best of all, selling yourself. One of the major reasons small businesses fail is because they do not know how to sell. There are businesses that may not have great products but they sell enough of it to stay afloat or even thrive. On the other hand, there are businesses that have great products but because of a poor sales team or strategy, they struggle or just crumble.

There are two reasons why people the world over buy anything. Most people think that the reason people buy things is that they need them or that they want them. People do not just buy things because they need it or want it. This is because most people do not even know what they need and even when some know what they need, they still do not buy it. If you are able to show them the value they will get from the product you are offering, you will find that people will buy. People will not buy things they are not comfortable with or do not know about.

The reason why people buy anything is more emotional than logical. People buy things to fulfil their passion or relieve a fear. If you can arouse that sense that you can fulfil either emotion, then people will buy from you. There have been whole industries built around these two emotions. It is not rocket science; it is simply a product of long term research or observation of human behaviour. You must segment your market and know who your product is targeting and which of the emotions you are addressing with what you are offering.

Cars meet the need for mobility. If people bought cars just based on need, which is mobility, everyone would just drive a Toyota or a Honda. But when you want to fulfil people's passion, you have to produce cars like Maserati, Rolls Royce, Bentley, Porsche etc.

Closely tied with your ability to sell is your ability to negotiate. Whether you are a big corporation signing mergers, acquisitions or hostile takeovers you must learn the basics and then the advanced skills for negotiation. This same is true for small businesses that more often than not have to come up with creative financing for their start-up, navigate the murky waters of dealing with suppliers, sub-contractors, partner companies and clients alike.

One ground rule in negotiations is to know "What is in it for them". You must understand the obvious and sometimes not so obvious issues that are at stake for a business negotiation. It is definitely a no-go situation when the person you are negotiating with has nothing at stake and has nothing to lose should the deal fall through.

The best negotiations end in a win-win situation for all the parties involved and if there is effective, open and enough communication between the parties, like in a high trust environment, it is possible to find a higher ground where the objectives of both parties are met.

The most important difference between entrepreneurs and those who never dare to make the leap is their thinking and that little difference makes all the difference in the outcomes. In this regard, technical or academic abilities play less critical roles in determining success or failure.

"Problems cannot be solved at the same level of thinking that created them"

Albert Einstein

Chapter Nine

WORKING HARD VS WORKING SMART

"Wealth is when small efforts produce big results. Poverty is where big efforts produce small results."

Author unknown

One of the most puzzling ironies I have seen in life is where a very smart person works for a very "un-smart" person. They may have multiple degrees from Ivy League schools, consider themselves very smart, work hard as horses, but at the end of the day, the boss is still the boss. It does not matter much what title you bear, what you wear or how long you stay in the office and how many people you order around, I am more concerned with who really pulls the string behind the stage or who the real boss is, period.

The hardest workers are not necessarily the best paid. For example, when you go to a construction site, the least paid workers are the hardest working. They are the unskilled and semi-skilled members of the workforce. While someone is sitting in their air-conditioned office, moving things up and down the page with his mouse, or these days, swiping his fingers across a screen, the unskilled workers are out there exposed to all the fury of nature as they haul tonnes of material up and down all day and yet, they earn a tiny fraction of what the skilled workers earn.

If given a choice, most people will always choose the easier and faster way of doing anything. When any advice comes along that promises this easier path, people are prone to take the advice particularly when it is a cliché. When people take the advice to work smart and not work hard, they try to find the best way to do whatever it is they have to do. They expect it will most likely make their life simpler. It is like trying to find the path of least resistance, or find the easiest way to get anything done. At face value, it does not seem so bad. As a matter of fact, it seems pretty good, like sound advice that everyone should take. Sadly, it might not be as safe as you think.

I think both working hard and working smart are two sides of the same coin. In today's contemporary world, smart work is always preferred over hard work partly because of this much publicized cliché, and the fact that we often do not tell the stories of the hard work of successful people or, when we do tell them, we extract all those bare knuckle, extended hours, sweat, grit and sheer exertion that culminated in their success. We often tell the stories of the brilliant ideas, plans, strategies and other smart moves as the precursor to their success.

We cannot achieve our ambition by choosing either hard work or smart work. To be our level best, we should accept both types of legerdemain. The one who wants to do smart work, would have to do hard work to be smart. Hence for some people and at certain times, hard work is more expedient than smart work. I know that hard work is time consuming and physically tasking but fact is fact and there are no shortcuts to becoming a success without hard work. Yet, you must know when to work hard and also how and when to work smart.

Working smart implies that you bring a lot of skill, talent, knowledge, expertise to bear instead of working hard with just raw power and physical exertion. One way to work smart is to always "sharpen your saw". Sharpening your saw means developing and refining the skills necessary to get your job done the best and fastest way possible. Imagine a man goes into the jungle to fell trees. Because of the urgency of the task, and his desire to cut down many trees, he skips the task of sharpening his saw. So he dives into the task and spends all his energy trying to cut as many trees as he can. In spite of his great effort, his effectiveness can be as low as 50%, compared to the man who sharpened his saw at the onset, and continues to sharpen his saw at regular intervals. So his effort yields greater return because his tools and methods are better. It was

Abraham Lincoln who said "If I had six hours to chop down a tree, I will spend the first four sharpening the axe"

A much more fundamental consideration is whether he should be cutting trees at all, and whether he should be cutting that particular bush. What a waste it would be, to spend your entire time, life, or career cutting trees, in the wrong forest whereas you should not be cutting trees at all, but planting trees in a different forest. This analogy is simple, yet it is applicable to the many things we do in life.

Another important consideration, most people fail to take into account is the sometimes subtle difference between "doing things right" and "doing the right things." It is easy for most people to tell the difference between right and wrong. The real problem comes with telling the difference between "doing the right things" and "doing things right". "Doing things right" is efficiency, but "doing the right things" is effectiveness. Before you undertake a task, and proceed to do it very well (efficiently), you must ask yourself whether you should do the task at all, whether it has any contribution to your long term goals and aspirations. They say "It is no use doing well what you should not be doing at all". Working smart helps you to identify what you should be working on so that you do not waste your energy working hard on the wrong things or as they say "sweating the small stuff".

Many people confuse activity with accomplishments. That a lot of energy was expended in no way means that something worthwhile was achieved. The person could just have been busy doing nothing.

The challenge with the advice "work smart and not hard" is that there are no easy ways to do some things, and getting to the comfortable altitude of "working smart" takes a lot of "hard work". So when people are not willing to do what it takes to get to that altitude, they short change themselves because they have believed a cliché that is not compatible with their present make-up and set-up, that is who they are and where they are now in relation to what they have to do to get to where they want to get to.

There are some folks who are pretty quick mentally. They may lack athleticism but they never had to put too much effort into scholastic advancement. If they saw it enough times not only could they remember the information, but they could also apply it to differing circumstances that seem to fit the same mould. They do not have a straight "A" brain with no studying but with minimal effort, they could stay in the "B+" to "A-" range and with extra effort, their straight A status will be cemented.

For these folks, elementary, middle, and high school, while socially not the easiest, was no issue academically. Even undergraduate studies were survivable while spending some of their nights up and out. They probably could have done better academically, but they figured that if they could get the B+ and catch up on some sleep, it wasn't the worst thing ever. When it reaches PhD level, you realize that the inborn smartness almost counts for nothing. It is those students who have developed a consistent work ethic that can come up with ideas and see their ideas through, prepare their thesis, defend them and get through the program.

People tend to think that the memorable people in our world are people born with talents. We look at their talent as if it were something we could never attain, as if it were something in their genes. In reality, the people who are most consistently successful are the ones who have become obsessive about their craft and have practiced it at a cost. And such disciplined practice takes a lot of hard work.

Work is important as it takes us to the next level of success. The most important question you should ask at every point in time is, " what kind of work will take you to that level: is it hard work or smart work?"
Malcolm Gladwell, author of Outliers, has clearly documented the science to back up these claims that talent is not enough. He refers to people who do not fit into our normal understanding of success as

outliers. One of the common themes in the book is the "10,000 hour rule". The idea is that greatness requires a lot of time – approximately 10,000 hours. He uses examples such as Bill Gates and the Beatles. Bill Gates put in programming time on a computer he had access to when he was in high school. The Beatles put in time in Hamburg, Germany performing over 1,200 times. He doesn't suggest that talent has no bearing at all; merely that talent or genius alone is not enough. The time you put in will show. Obviously, if you like doing something and have a knack for it, you will be more likely to put the time and hard work into it.

My basic understanding of the Chinese yin yang philosophy in its simplest form is based on the ability to hold two opposing views and yet be able to function. Working hard "OR" working smart has created a dichotomy and opposing schools of thought that immobilizes some people. What if we replace the "OR" with "AND", so that instead of choosing one of working hard "OR" working smart, we come up with a third option which is a combination of working hard "AND" working smart.

I am both for hard work and smart work. For those who always want to advocate for working smart, my simple question for them is: do you know how much hard work it takes to work smart? You must first understand where you are at a point in time and know what is required of you. It makes no sense working hard when you should be working smart or vice versa. Actually hard work and smart work go hand in hand for you to be successful. Smart work is about making the right strategy. Smart work always saves you time which is an important aspect. Through smart work you can achieve your goals faster.

However, hard work is the building block for smart work. To do smart work, one should have sound knowledge of the subject. This knowledge can be achieved only through hard work. In these days, you hear a lot of talk about working smart. People often tell you, "You don't get anywhere by sheer hard work. Look at the people working at construction sites. They are working very hard, but are they getting anywhere in life? If you want to achieve success, you need to work smart." Such comments leave some of us in confusion. What happens to sayings like, "Work hard and the success will be yours"?

Success is often a result of hard work. But it's important to recognize that failure, too, is often a result of hard work. As entrepreneurs, we must recognize the difference between working hard and working smart; not just for ourselves, but for those we lead. Here is a simple truth: working hard on the wrong things does not make one successful. Like we said before, too many people work hard at making sure that they are doing things right, but fail to consider first whether they are doing the right things.

So the simple advice I can give you would be to "work smart and work hard" with a caveat -this advice is selectively applicable. You must determine when to work hard and when to work smart or do both based on your peculiar circumstances and what you intend to achieve.

WORK HARDER ON YOURSELF THAN ON YOUR JOB

Jim Rohn once said, "Work harder on yourself than you do on your job. If you work hard on your job you can make a living. If you work hard on yourself you can make a fortune." After all, we can only grow our businesses as to the extent we grow ourselves. We all grow older in age, but growing in critical areas as an individual is optional. It is a choice you and only you can make. Every experience, thought, relationship and encounter in life gives us the opportunity to grow, whether a negative or positive experience. The reason why most do not commit to daily growth is because it requires you to move out of your comfort zone. You cannot grow while you are comfortable. Growing as an individual can include learning a new skill, refining an old one, changing your thought process, reading more or waking up earlier than normal and this will require you to move past your comfort zone.

When you are doing a start-up, or working a great job, it is often hard to separate life and work. Therefore, why not work away on yourself just like you do on your start-up or job? Plan the necessary disengagement from the start-up just as carefully as you would plan the time you work on it. If you can systematically improve and expand your skills, then whether a start-up or job works out or not, you will always be in an increasingly better position as the weeks and months pass. This does not mean that you do not give 100% to your work, it just means to focus 100% on yourself first, the value then that you bring to your job or business or family increases hundred-fold. The more you work on yourself, the better things get in every sphere of your life.

Self-Examination

The first step to working on yourself is a thorough self-assessment. This is not about looking in the mirror and asserting that everything is great. As someone wise said: "The biggest room in the world is the room for improvement". This does not undermine your strengths, but to enhance those strengths, you need to focus very specifically on what things you need to improve on – is it your self-confidence, your ability to plan and be organized, your financial skills, your marketing or networking skills, your writing or speaking skills? Identify the areas and drill down further to the "how". We are lucky to have amazing resources available in books and on the internet on any topic that you could think of and many support groups to help you on to achievement.

Be a Life-Long Learner

What has been is not anymore. What is will not be forever. What is to come, is not here yet. Do not restrict learning to the four walls of a school. Make the world your school. Lifelong learners tend to love what they do, or they at least find some aspect of it to love. Learners love the challenge, if nothing else. It is the learners who question the status quo, shake things about and are innovators. And of course getting rewarded at their jobs or business is an inevitable side benefit as learning keeps you current and relevant. There are two parts to learning – staying current and learning a new skill. Set some time aside for reading. There are books on just about any topic, there is so much information also on the internet, there is a plethora of magazines and blogs that you can subscribe to, you can definitely find an article that captures your interest or simply browse through the archives. Learning a new skill will help you expand your capabilities and keep your mind sharp.

Be Yourself, Be Your Best Self

Realize that you are in control of yourself. We all have our own standards of excellence. We also have different priorities, and what motivates me to put in 100% won't necessarily be the same for you. Whatever your own standard of excellence is in your work, whatever you feel passionately about – that is what you should be true to. Do not stop doing or keep doing stuff just because some of your colleagues' standards of excellence are lower than yours or their priorities are different. Your measuring stick for your own achievement should be based on what you want to achieve, not how much or little other people are doing. What excites you most? Feed that passion and find ways to align it with your work responsibilities. They say "imitation is limitation". The best person you can ever be is yourself, but remaining who you are today will limit who you can be tomorrow. Every day, through every trial and triumph, seek to create an improved and custom-made version of yourself.

Avoid the Negative(And Reinforce the Positive)

What makes you feel tired and drained – it could be people, thoughts or activities. If you want to maintain a positive attitude, consider sharply limiting your daily exposure to such experiences. Don't show up at the daily complaint sessions at work. If you have got family members or friends who are constantly negative, tune them out. Your happiness lies within you – trite but true, practice happiness every day, make it your sacred ritual. No matter what you do for a living, the key to success is great performance, every single day. And that is only possible if you make optimism, energy, and enthusiasm part of your daily experience. Avoid toxic people, relationships, jobs etc.; they simply leave you drained with nothing worthwhile to show for it.

Help Others Succeed

A Zulu proverb says, "Umuntu ngumuntu ngabantu" (A human is only a human because of other humans). We are all interconnected! Your Success is assured and becomes more meaningful when you help others succeed. Personal relationships are the fertile soil from which all advancement, all success, all achievement in real life grows. The more you give of yourself in anything, the more you get in return – especially when you give with no expectation of return. Too often, we build islands for ourselves cutting ourselves off from people who we can learn from, grow and share life's experiences with. Do what you can for other people, work hard at building relationships. It is a sure-fire way to help you become a personal and professional success and live a fulfilling life.

It Usually Takes A Few Tries

There is truly nothing like overnight success. Most successful entrepreneurs get it right after a lot of tries. A proof of your experience as an entrepreneur is when you go into your next venture as an improved version of you. It is insane to make the same mistake over and over again, hoping that mother luck will shine on you and turn your mess into something else. Even if you lose money in a venture, do not lose the experience, let the money serve as tuition in the University of Life.

Build Your Network

In a later chapter "VIP Only", we will explore the fact that people will make or break your business. You can never overestimate the power of people. From family, neighbours, colleagues, employers, employees, clients, and even friends of friends, you must build your network. Your network will ultimately determine your net worth.

Exercise and Pay Attention to Your Body

Your health is very important and it is your sole responsibility to take care of your body. You must create time to exercise. You must observe good eating habits, rest and sleep adequately. It takes a lot of discipline to maintain healthy habits but it is better to endure the pain of discipline than that of regret.

Keep in Touch

Know what is going on in your field and where your field is going to. You will be left behind if you think things will remain the same. These are the days of accelerated change and you should always be up to speed. If you are not the one leading the change, at least keep pace, you cannot afford to be left behind. What has been will not always be, and what will be, is not here yet.

Be an Expert at Something

You cannot afford to remain a "jack of all trades and master of none". Curiosity is an indispensible attribute of an entrepreneur, but you cannot always have your hand in every pie. There is a time to know a little of everything, it will aid you when you are still thinking of what to focus on. A time must come when you will progress and seek to know everything about something. That is mastery and quantum success is only possible at this level of mastery. Mastery here does not just refer to the mastery of a skill or in a field; it is much more a mastery of yourself.

"Hard work beats talent when talent doesn't work hard".
Tim Notke

Chapter Ten

BEST KEPT SECRET

"I firmly believe that any man's finest hour, the greatest fulfilment of all that he holds dear, is that moment when he has worked his heart out in a good cause and lies exhausted on the field of battle - victorious."

Vince Lombardi

One of the ironies of life is that some people indulge in practices or vices that are harmful to them. A similar tragedy is when people avoid things that are beneficial to them and may be engaging instead in detrimental practices.

WORK

I have come to realize that the best kept secret about work is that work is good for you. I do want to consider this submission right from the very start. When I look at the creation story, I can see clearly that God gave man work before the fall and the resultant curse. So work is not a product of the fall, but an integral part of the awesome masterpiece we call our universe.

Another noteworthy fact is that God gave man work before he gave him Eve. I see where Foxy Brown got her lyrics "You've got to have a "JOB" if you wanna be with me". Finally, it is encouraging for me to see that help came (in the form of the woman) as a necessary requirement for the task man had to undertake. The help you receive in an endeavour is usually commensurate with the size of the undertaking. So if you choose to do nothing, you do not need any help to do that. They say, "Nothing goes for nothing".

Work will not kill you, it will actually make you live longer. Some people see their work like it is killing. This is not because of the work but a product of a wrong mind-set and attitude regarding work. When my dad retired after over thirty five years in public service, we (his children) figured that we could afford to take care of his upkeep, so he should just get a recliner, kick off his socks and chill and sip martinis all day. We could take care of all his upkeep even if he does not get his pension or earn a dime more. In hindsight, I am glad an uncle talked us out of our plan in its entirety. He counselled us to give him all the support he needed, but that we should not stop him from working. He has kept himself busy in new pursuits, ventures and pastimes and he is better for it. This is far from suggesting that we live to work; rather I am saying that we work to live.

When people cease working, they lose the benefit of exercising their physical and mental faculties and like unused muscles, they begin to atrophy.

Retirement is no excuse; you can dream new dreams at old age. Colonel Harland Sanders started KFC at the age of sixty five, when some of his peers where packing their bags waiting for the undertaker. He is a "finger lickin good" example of flourishing in old age.

If you were offered everything you have ever desired in life now without working for it, will you take it? Remember the old story of someone seeing a magic lamp, rubbing the lamp and then the genie comes out to grant their wish? If the genie grants your wish, everything you have ever desired will fall on your lap. Trust me pals, if everything you have ever desired falls on your lap, it will break you. No man has the capacity to take that much at once. If you come into such utopia without adequate mental preparation, it will ruin you. It is like the waters of the ocean flowing into a swimming pool. That is a tsunami, and more than getting the water you desire, it will leave monumental destruction in its wake because the pool does not have the capacity to hold all the water in the ocean.

When you grow incrementally, you learn the ropes and develop character in obscurity before you come into the spotlight. You know yourself before the world gets to know you and the process prepares you for what is prepared for you.

Why is it that many people who win the lottery go broke a few years after? Many of them end up worse than they were before. However, I know many millionaires who lose all their fortune, some even declare bankruptcy, yet many of them make the money over again. The reason is that they have learned the best kept secret, work.

The bible says in Proverbs 14:23 and 10:4 (The Message Version); Hard work always pays off; mere talk puts no bread on the table; Sloth makes you poor; diligence brings wealth.

Wise millionaires use this secret when grooming their children or successors. In the classic book-'Built to Last', Jim Collins and Jerry Porras showed through their extensive research that most companies that last long get their CEOs from within the organization. This concept is not lost on these wise entrepreneurs. But it is instructive to note that most of them do not take their protégé and give him an office next to the pent house suite. They send the protégée to the very bottom of the chain or as an intern in another establishment so they can learn the essence of work or the workings of the entire organization they aspire to sit over. They teach them to work, roll up their sleeves, get in the trenches; whatever it takes, if need be, kind of training.

Early in the last century, the famous billionaire John D. Rockefeller, Jr. taught his children the value of money using a simple process. He taught them the necessity for work, the importance of charity, the need for saving and the power of accountability

John D. Rockefeller, Jr., was certainly not trying to save money when he decided to give allowances to his five sons and they had to earn the rest. To earn extra money, one of his sons raised vegetables and rabbits. All the boys were required to keep personal daily account books. They were required to give 10 per cent of their income to charity, to save 10 per cent, and to account for all the rest. They had to balance their account books every month and to be able to tell what happened to every penny they earned. His son Nelson went on to serve as Governor of the state of New York for many years, and, ultimately, became Vice President of the United States. One of his brothers, David Rockefeller, Chairman of the Chase Manhattan Bank, said, "We all profited by the experience-especially when it came to understanding the value of money".

The importance of work cannot be over-emphasized. Even natural talents fail without work. This is true for musicians, athletes and anyone for that matter. By working, taking massive action, you set yourself up for massive results.

Work helps us discover the potential on the inside of each of us. And we expand our capacity by exerting ourselves. It is much like working out in a gym. Someone once said that you cannot develop your muscles by having someone else "work out" for you. You develop your physical and mental muscles by "working out" by yourself. You sometimes never know what you can do till you try.

Work brings a satisfaction to us that we cannot get via any other means. It is our opportunity to make a contribution to humanity, advance the course of humanity and make the world a better place. Refusal to work robs the world of your unique contribution. So you are not the only loser in the equation.

Sometimes we take for granted all the advancements in technology, healthcare, education and many other spheres of our lives. When you consider the work previous generations put in to get us to where we are today, then you know that we should not let the "labour of our heroes past" be in vain and you owe posterity your contribution to the advancement of our common humanity.

WHO DO YOU WORK FOR?

Who do you work for? When people are asked this question, they often call the name of their boss or whoever they consider their employer. One realization that has revolutionised my life is that everybody works for himself. Even if you are not self-employed, you still work for yourself.

It is obvious that business owners put in more work, both in quality and quantity particularly for start-ups and small concerns. It is easy to deduce that it is because they are working for themselves. If you realise too that whoever you are and wherever you work, that you are working for yourself, do you think that you will do a better job?

Why is it that self-employed people or entrepreneurs do not do the nine-to-five or the forty or forty eight hour-week working schedules? It is definitely because they know that they are working for themselves. Why do employees put in an eight hour shift without putting anything into the shift? Because they think that they are working for their boss.

Who are you really working for? Most people have never sat down to really consider this question. They work for thirty five years or more and they do not even know who they are working for. One of the secrets of work is that you work for yourself; you do not work for your boss. That shift is enough to take your career through the roof. You really do work for yourself.

You went to school, took all the time and money, some on loan, to acquire the skill and competence. Then you bring that to the table and lay your life down (your time is your life, even if you call it your time) to do the work. And you take home the pay at the end of the month and spend it on what you will. So who are you working for? Your boss or yourself? If you are the one who receives and spends the proceeds of your work, then you really are working for yourself. If you do not get that, you will be lazy about your work, remain stuck on your pay check all your life and never get a chance to live the life of your dream.

The best kept secret about work is that whatever the garb, façade, definition or description, ultimately, YOU WORK FOR YOURSELF AND WORK IS GOOD FOR YOU.

Work is not a punishment or a burden. Work is an opportunity to be part of the creative process. Work is an expression of your inherent endowment as an individual. Work gives you a chance to be part of the privileged few who are actively making our world a better place to live in. Dr. Myles Munroe said, "A man should be afraid to die if he has not done anything worth remembering him for".

TGIF is a popular slogan among employees and some people trudge through their work day for closing time; they cling onto the ropes to make it to the end of the day till they are saved by the bell. They call it nine-to-five, simply marking time. They cannot wait for Friday so that they can take a break from the burden called work. Even some play the religious card that God rested on the seventh day as the basis for their rest. What they do not consider is that God worked his socks off six days of the week before taking a well-earned rest on the seventh day. So why do you want to take the weekend off when you have not done anything tangible all week long?

When work is a pleasure, life is a joy! When work is a duty, life is slavery.

Maxim Gorky

Chapter Eleven

TIME AND MONEY

Let him who would enjoy a good future waste none of his present.

Roger Babson

Is this chapter a detour? I thought we were talking about entrepreneurship? How come we are talking about time? I have had many people tell me once and again, "I want to make money" and I see these same people squander their time away day after day and many years down the road, they wonder why they are not any closer to their goal of making money. The answer to their riddle is time. If I could teach the whole world one thing, I would teach the world the value of time and how to manage time. Whatever you desire to attain or acquire in life, give it enough time and you will get it. But the challenge is that we do not have all the time in the world to do what we need to do in the world.

People have dreams, goals, aspirations, desires and visions. The greatest frustration in life often stems from these desires not being accomplished with time. People expect time to deliver their dreams into their laps, yet they procrastinate taking necessary actions. One of the greatest deceptions people have believed is that things change with time. So in time, they believe that the things they desire will come to them, not true at all. Even in waiting, they say that "good things come to those who hustle while they wait". People change things in time, if things are to change as desired. Some people set goals in a particular area of their life, but they spend their time in just about every other endeavour but what will move them in the direction of their goals. And the years go by and they wonder why they are not any closer to their dreams.

I have this contraption of quotes I used for effect some time ago. *"Dreams still come true, if you want them bad enough. In order to have good dreams, do not sleep with people who have nightmares and for your dreams to come true, wake up".*

Wake up and start to work on your dreams with all the time you have got.

A very pertinent question that stirred my thoughts for a long time was the question: Which is more important, time or money? The answer came simply from analysing the relationship the rich and the poor have with time and money. It will take weeks to walk from Abuja to Lagos. About ten hours by road and less than an hour by air. Why do the rich part with much money to make the trip the fastest way possible. Is it to save time? Or are they just living in the fast lane? Everything you get in life is a trade-off. A trade-off is what you are willing to give in order to get what you want? And every trade-off is a measure of value. We do not just trade off, we try to trade up. We always give what we value less, to get what we value more. The rich spend money to save time; the poor spend time to save money. If then the rich trade money for time, what is of more value, time or money? To the rich, the obvious answer is that they value their time more than money.

Earlier, I measured the distance between the city of Abuja and Lagos in terms of time. Depending on your purse or rather your mentality, the distance between Abuja and Lagos maybe one hour (by air), ten hours (by land) or ten weeks (by foot). It is actually possible via technology to further shrink this time to almost nothing. I mean a phone call, an email, or better still, teleconferencing. This is as good as a face to face conversation.

Everything we have in life is a trade-off of something else. If some were born with more talents, beauty and brains or inherited a fortune, then the deck would have been stacked against some others right from the start. They say "it is not the hand that life deals you, but it is how you play the hand that matters". The real things that set men apart are not what we are endowed with at birth or the good winds or ill winds we may encounter on life's journey, but it is what we do therein and thereafter. For example, there are people who inherited mega-fortunes and ended up paupers soon after. Many have been born talented, but ended as fitting examples of what should have been. Yet, many born poor have become first generation millionaires. It is clear that talent is not enough, skill must be honed. Discipline must be learnt.

For me, death is the greatest motivator in life. The reason for this is that at death, time is no more. The dead have run out of time. They may have money, houses, streets named after them, legacies or businesses with their names, friends and foes alike, but they do not have time anymore. They cannot play any part in the affairs of the living. And their whole life is summed up in a short hyphen between two intervals of time, 1930-2015. And that brief interval is actually our time, our life. Thus the measure of our life is the time we spend here. Does that mean that our time is our life? Is our time as important, less important or more important than our life?

Why is our life called "Life Time"? If our life is our time, then the quality of the use of our time determines the quality of our life. What you trade your time for, determines what you will get in life. The value you place on your time, will determine the value you will have in life. If you do not place value on your time, others will as well not value your time.

How much you understand time, will determine how much you understand life. Anybody or anything that wastes your time is wasting your life.

Time is inelastic, irreplaceable, and irrecoverable. It cannot be stopped, turned back or held back. It will keep ticking whether you kick or you stand still. It will not wait for anyone or run fast because of another. Every human being gets an equal portion daily. The difference between each one at the end of the day is how much value we placed on our time. What we traded our time for, in the course of the day. Time is not a cycle like day and night; it is a continuum, an interruption in eternity.

There is a lot of academic intelligence out there and people are doing their best to acquire financial intelligence; so many people telling you how to invest your money in varied schemes and for various returns. I am developing a new field I refer to as "Timepreneur". It is the act of investing time, the most valuable commodity you have in life for a return here and for eternity.

Life is measured in time. I have also realised that even in astronomy, distance is measured in time. The scientist measures small distances like the diameter of the earth in regular units like kilometre. But when the scientists have to deal with gargantuan proportions like the size of our galaxy, they must resort to measurement in terms of time. That is why they use the term, "light years".

What if everything in life is denominated by time? What if we measure and evaluate everything in life by time? What if value and importance were not just based on the apparent but the time tested value inherent in anything? Even the true value of money is predicated on time. The effect of investment, return on investments and inflation implies that the true value of money is predicated on time.

All God ever gave us was time, and all he will ever give is time. Our results in life are based on what we choose to trade our time for. Nobody came to this world an expert at anything, whether financial management, football, golf, music or just anything else. Some showed up with a measure of talent but like it has been shown again and again, it is not only "America's got talent" or "Britain's got talent", the whole world's got talent. And trading your time for training and skill acquisition and perfection is what sets apart champions, winners and MVPs from others who just had talent.

Some people were born with talents, but nobody was born with skills. Talent must be honed with time and then it becomes skill. Everyone was born without a language; we traded time and learned one, two, three or more languages depending on how much time we were willing to trade. Even nuclear physicists were not born with Einstein's laws inside their DNA. They had to first grapple with even the basic physics, and then the Newtonian laws till they acquired the advanced knowledge with time.

You can get anything in life that you are willing to trade enough time for. It is obvious that time is more important than money, just like life, but very few people truly realise this. If they did, they would not waste time. To waste your time is to waste your life. People have been known to have made fortunes, then lose them either by bad decisions or any other reason. And many have been known to have made the fortune back. You can get more money, but you can never get more time.

TIME MANAGEMENT

From our earlier discuss, if time is as important as we have opined, then, managing it will be a most critical ingredient for success. There are so many schools of thought, techniques, strategies, planners (PDAs and day, week or year planner) and much more on time management. From what to do when you wake, to how to have your lunch, all through what to do last thing before you go to bed, to how long you should sleep, there are different ideas on how to manage your time effectively. Some are absolutely outlandish. Yet, for all the others, the advocates have tried them with various levels of success. Though people may promote their brand of time management technique and tools, it is really your choice based on what works for you. The bottom line is that you must manage your time properly, but there is no one rule fits all for time management. You may have to adopt different strategies for different phases of your life, but the ground rule for me is; whatever works for you, work it.

Time management is something many people struggle with. The secret to managing your time effectively is knowing what you want to do and when you will do it. This way, you stay proactive and in "execute" mode rather than reactive in "catch up" mode. But managing your time is easier said than done. Good time management requires an important shift in focus from activities to results: being busy is not the same as being effective.

What is "Time Management?"

"Time management" refers to the way that you organize and plan how long you spend on specific activities.

It may seem counter-intuitive to dedicate precious time to learning about time management, instead of using it to get on with your work, but the benefits are enormous. They include:

- Greater productivity and efficiency.
- A better professional reputation.

- Less stress and more fulfilment.
- Increased opportunities for advancement.
- Greater opportunities to achieve important life and career goals.

Failing to manage your time effectively can have some very undesirable consequences. They include:

- Missed deadlines.
- Inefficient work flow.
- Poor work quality.
- A poor professional reputation and a stalled career.
- Higher stress levels.

Time is one of life's most valuable possessions, as it is something you can never get back. Subsequently, one of the most essential life skills to master is time management. After all, time management is really life management. Learning how to make every day count for something is the objective. But it takes ridding your life of procrastination and a great deal of self-discipline. Mastering time management does more than just increase productivity. It can yield important health benefits as well. When time is managed wisely, it minimizes stress and improves the overall quality of your life.

PRINCIPLES OF TIME MANAGEMENT

Some of the basic principles of time management include:

1. Have a purpose.

Purpose is the reason for the creation or existence of anything. Purpose offers clarity and direction. It generates the energy you need to be productive because it is something you believe in. It is much easier to work towards something when we know what that "something" is. Additionally, a purpose offers feedback as it summons you back towards true north when your behaviour begins to fall off course. To identify what drives you, ask yourself where you enjoy spending time compared to where you must spend your time. Are they the same? If not, it may be time to realign. Having a purpose helps you when you are planning your time. You allocate your most productive time to the activities that will move you in the direction of your purpose.

2. Have a plan.

Without a plan for your day, your day can go in any direction and at the end of the day; your sense of accomplishment will be fuzzy because there is no benchmark to compare your day's accomplishment against.

This plan can be as simple as a daily, weekly and maybe monthly to-do list. It is a very simple yet profoundly useful tool for time management. When you check things off your list, it releases a sense of pleasure and accomplishment that spurs you on to achieve more. It helps you to identify the most important tasks of your day and if they are arranged in the order of their priority, you start with the most important item and work your way down the list.

Besides a "to do" list, you can have a "not to do" list, even if it is not written. These are things that are not critical to your purpose. They are things you can defer, delegate, outsource or leave doing them altogether.

Any activity or conversation that is important to your success should have a time assigned to it. Do not let your to-do lists get longer and longer to the point where they are unworkable. Some advocate creating your to-do list last thing at night, so that your sub-conscious mind will start to work on it overnight. Others advocate doing it first thing in the morning when your mind is clear. Whichever works for you, do it, just be sure you have a plan for your day.

Appointment books work for some people. Schedule appointments with yourself and create time blocks for high-priority thoughts, conversations, and actions. Schedule when each activity will begin and end. Have the discipline to keep these appointments.

Having a plan helps you to know what to say yes or no to. Saying no to distractions and non-essentials frees your time for the truly important things that you should be occupying yourself with.

3. Use Your Free Time

There are only three ways to spend time: thoughts, conversations and actions. Regardless of the type of business you own, your work will be composed of those three items. If you drive to work, how do you pass the time during your commute? If you take a bus or train, how do you spend all those hours a week? How many audiobooks or language tapes could you have completed while in traffic last month? How many books could you read on the train while getting to and from work the next few weeks?

These are the best times throughout your day to incorporate all those little things that you "wished" you had time for. Over time, these habits become a lifestyle, and you will find yourself well ahead of the pack.

4. Be predictable.

When urgencies arise, they throw your daily routine out of whack because the tasks you planned on finishing get pushed to the back burner. You can remedy this by creating a set schedule for when you will do certain things like check email, workout or socialize. The more predictability you can introduce into your schedule, the more opportunities you will be aware of where you can accommodate urgencies when they arise.

Chances are good that, at some time in your life, you have taken a time management class, read about it in books, and tried to use an electronic or paper-based day planner to organize, prioritize and schedule your day. Many people have tried these different things and some have concluded that they do not work. The simple problem is that you must find one which works for you. That is why some advocate self-management instead of time management. You cannot manage time effectively if you do not know yourself well and thus cannot manage yourself in time. If you do not find one that works for you out there, you can create your own.

5. Avoid distractions

As an entrepreneur, you may be frequently interrupted or pulled in different directions. While you cannot eliminate interruptions, you do have a say on how much time you will spend on them and how much time you will spend on the thoughts, conversations and actions that will lead you to success.

I once heard Dr. Myles Munroe say that "distraction by good people is a bad idea". We can get a lot more done if we put work into all the time we put into work. Very often, people are distracted by many things that are not part of their schedule, but just crop up to clog their time.

Practice not answering the phone just because it is ringing and e-mails just because they show up.

Disconnect instant messaging if it becomes a distraction. Do not instantly give people your attention unless it is absolutely crucial in your business to offer an immediate human response. Instead, schedule a time to answer email and return phone calls.

Block out other distractions like Facebook and other forms of social media unless you use these tools to generate business.

6. Never hesitate to take a break if needed.

Everyone gets worn out from time to time and piling on more and more tasks leads to stress that will simply derail you from the mission at hand. Take a walk, go to the gym, get some fresh air or take that sick day or leave that you have been holding out on. Sometimes all we need is a moment of clarity and solitude to clear our overworked minds and recharge our bodies to give us that next big push.

INVESTMENTS

The world has gone through many dispensations such as the agrarian age, the industrial age, and now, it is called the information age. Information is all around us in many diverse formats. The general assumption should be that if information is so pervasive around us, everyone should be a walking encyclopaedia. In spite of the wealth of information around us, we have created a generation ignorant of certain things just like a generation that lived through the dark ages when there was the dearth of information.

Most of the information that we are bombarded with every day is information that is mostly irrelevant to life. People are fed every day with a whole lot of entertainment, music, fun and the likes, which leave the learner no better equipped to face today's challenges.

The principles of life are not for the casual learner. It is reserved for those who seek beyond the surface to find the meaning to the seeming madness and a way through the maze called life.

One area that people are so ignorant about is money. Some go through the cycle of 'earn and spend' without ever stopping to ask some fundamental questions about money. Yet they spend the useful part of their entire existence chasing this elusive money without ever stopping to ask themselves, what is this all about? Some earn, spend some, save some and invest mostly through a third party in an investment scheme they know absolutely or next to nothing about.

One of the most important ground rules about investment that I think will serve every investor is to be well informed about what ever area you want to invest in. There are many portfolios that can generate good return on investment, yet like they say in the stock market, there are bulls, and there are bears, and usually, the bears get slaughtered. I remember a time when suddenly, everyone around me was investing in the stock market. There was a serious feeding frenzy and every IPO then was oversubscribed. People sold lands, houses and borrowed money with different interest rates all to invest in shares. And invest in shares they did.

Most of these people had no clear understanding of the workings of the stock market. Some simply handed over their money to the stock broker who broke their heart in due time. Some expected to invest what they were investing and reap immediate gains, say at the end of the year. When the bubble burst, it was a sorry sight to see some of these people crying over huge losses and debts.

Then these same people will suddenly gravitate to the other end of the pole, and start to tell everyone that so and so investment is a bad investment. Yet, there have been and there will always be people who make monies from these same types of investment portfolios. The difference is the level of knowledge of the investor in the area he is investing in. Generally, there are no good or bad investments; there are only good or bad investors.

If you are getting financial advice, you must know from whom you are getting it. It was Warren Buffet who said that Wall Street is the only place where people ride a Rolls Royce to go and take financial advice from people who ride the subway. It is an irony for a millionaire to take financial advice from an office clerk on minimum wage or worse still, those who earn a commission based on how many people they can sucker.

Financial literacy is a must for anyone who wants to create lasting wealth and get out of the rat race of working for money. There are very many people who are educated and may have multiple degrees but they do not know anything about money. They spend all their lives working for money, but they do not understand what money is or how money works.

Would it make things better if we took all the money in the world and divided it equally among everyone? That would level the playing field and we would all live happily ever after, right? Wrong! It's been said that if you took all the money in the world and divided it up equally to everyone, before long, all the money will end up right back where it started in the first place; in the hands of the rich!

Why is that statement true? It is true because most people do not know what to do with their money, except spend it. Most people blow their pay check while keeping their fingers crossed hoping for the best. Managing and multiplying money is a skill that can be learned. Creating money as well is a skill that the rich have perfected.

Money is simply a reward for solving a problem by creating a product or a service. So if all the money in the world were divided equally, some people will just go out there and start to spend. And those who have learnt how to create value either as a product or a service will put these products out there, offer them to the spenders and get all the money back in no time.

According to Bob Proctor, "There are three income earning strategies. The first is trading time for money which is by far the worst of the three income earning strategies. It is employed by approximately 96% of our population including doctors, lawyers, accountants, labourers, etc. There are some inherent problems with this strategy – one is saturation, that is every other person has time too, equal amounts for that matter, and there is nothing different from your time and that of every other person. Another inherent problem is that you run out of time. If a person accumulates any degree of wealth employing this strategy, it will be at the expense of a life. They compromise on the car they drive, the house they live in, the clothes they choose and the vacations they take. They rarely, if ever, get what they want.

The second is investing money to earn money: this strategy is used by approximately 3% of the population. The number is small for the obvious reason – very few people have any money to invest and even fewer people have in-depth knowledge of investing. Financial intelligence is a must for anybody who wants to increase his net worth through this strategy. Academic intelligence falls flat in the face of financial matters at this level. Many people who effectively employ this strategy follow the advice of a trusted, knowledgeable advisor. Yet this is a risky venture, because sometimes, your advisor is more interested in his commission for example than if you actually get good return on your investment or not. One critical case in point is the stock market; where your stock broker can make his commission whether the value of the stock goes up or down. While the stock owner may be losing money, the broker still makes money. So the best bet is to have enough knowledge of whatever you want to invest in. Financial intelligence is an important acquisition besides all else.

And lastly, leveraging yourself to earn money: This is where you multiply your time through the efforts of others by setting up Multiple Streams of Income (MSI). This is, without question, the very best way to increase your income. For most people, the idea of multiple streams of income will be a powerful paradigm shift of immense proportions.

This concept is the strategy that wealthy people have used dating clearly back to the ancient Babylonians. Unfortunately, this strategy is only used by approximately 1% of our population, yet that 1% earns approximately 96% of all the money that is earned!

MULTIPLE STREAMS OF INCOME (MSI)

Multiple Streams of Income (MSI) is a concept, which has been adopted by almost all very wealthy people. It is exactly what it says; it is "income from multiple streams." Most employees earn income from only their job. Even some entrepreneurs have only one source of income. This is not only risky in our present economic clime but it is not a ready path to wealth creation. I believe in the power of focus, but in this context, we must focus on the result (wealth creation, financial freedom) instead of being stuck up on a single vehicle.

MSI is not simply another job, like working two or three jobs, neither is it a better job. Multiple Streams of Income is other source(s) of income aside your primary source of income. MSI is a way of adding a new dimension of excitement and fun to your everyday life, while you are becoming wealthy. One of the beauties of MSI is that not all require a huge capital outlay or acquisition of new skills; you can use your skill, hobby, interests, talents or existing assets. You create the MSI from what already exists.

Most people, employers and employees have a primary source of income. Yet, as humans, we are endowed with so many gifts, talents, have acquired skills and have opportunities that we can readily explore to create other streams of income.

The easiest way to create an MSI is to look at your immediate environment. Explore your skills and talent and find opportunities where you can convert them into a business model. Your MSI has to be such that instead of investing your time continuously, you can leverage yourself. This is where you multiply your time through the efforts of others by setting up business systems that can run themselves without your ever present time input. This is, without question, the very best way to increase your income.

One of the benefits of setting up MSI is that money comes into your pocket in so many ways; you do not depend on one source of income and thereby you avoid risk. You are practicing the art of diversification by not putting all your eggs in one basket, and you are leveraging your time. You can create some products, programs or services only once, and then market them over and over again.

Another benefit is that you get to explore all your skills and talents and even your innate abilities and untapped potentials and opportunities. Once you have one stream running, it frees you to focus on creating other streams.

Your MSI can be home-based or run from the same facility as your existing business, though not every business needs a physical address to operate. There are many millionaires from home-based businesses.

A common model of MSI is multi-level marketing or network marketing. There are many good ones out there as there are bad ones. Before you join any or commit your funds, please be sure to do your independent investigation. You cannot simply take the word of the recruiter in making your decision.

By starting multiple businesses, you are doing more than creating wealth for yourself; you are creating jobs, creating wealth for others and solving problems.

Another amazing benefit of MSI is that for an employee or even an entrepreneur, what started as just an extra stream of income can grow and become a major source of income. People have been known to resign their day job or change businesses completely because their "side gig" has become the real deal.

The major downside is that if care is not taken, you will tend to lose focus because you may be pulled in many different directions at the same time. If this becomes the case, sell off the businesses you can sell, close those that are proving unproductive or requiring too much time investment and focus on the ones that are healthy, growing or have potentials for growth.

Here are some popular general streams of income of most millionaires today:

- Real Estate - rental income, home appreciation, proceeds from sales;
- Financial Markets - stocks, bonds, money market accounts, etc.
- Business - brick and mortar or Internet based
- Freelancing as a journalist, writer, editor etc.
- Others are writing a book, giving talks, or trainings or making presentations, Social Media, Information Technology, TV Presentation, Branding, Public Relations, Selling Information Products and Services, Internet Marketing, Publishing, Event Hosting, Workshop facilitation, Event Planning, Musician, Poet, MC, Comedian, Photography, Makeup Artist, Catering services, Rental Services, etc.

This list is by no means exhaustive. You can turn your interest, hobby, passion, talent or skill into income streams if you do not have the money to go into real estate, financial market or business. Whatever it is you decide to do, do it now. Do not procrastinate. If you wait, you may wait forever.

If you love life, don't waste time, for time is what life is made up of."

— *Bruce Lee*

Chapter Twelve

YES, I DO

"Bad times have a scientific value. These are occasions a good learner would not miss."

— *Ralph Waldo Emerson*

Starting a business is a lot like getting married. Some jump in with no fore thought. Others stay on the side lines till all the waters in the rivers run dry. In marriage, most people are overly concerned about finding the right person without giving thought to being or becoming the right person, which is within their sphere of control. The most important ingredient in starting a business as it is in a successful relationship is the persons involved. You may have a million dollar idea, a winning business plan, a huge lump of cash and favourable external circumstances, but if the person is not 'up to it', they will reduce the business to their level. It was Abraham Maslow who said "if all you have is a hammer, everything looks like a nail." If you are not the person, you can become the person. Entrepreneurial skills can be learned just like other skills in life. I am yet to meet an entrepreneur described as talented or born as an entrepreneur.

Imagine that you are in a smooth sailing ship going nowhere. For most people, that is the story of their job, smooth sailing but not taking them where they want to go, not as fast as they want to get there and worst of all, they are not enjoying the ride. For a few people, the ride maybe turbulent, but jumping ship is something you must give deep contemplation to, except you can walk on water. You have to prepare a life jacket or a similar contingency plan because no one might take you back on board should you start to go under after jumping ship.

Maybe you have been working or job hunting but, have not found an ideal job that showcases your talents, education and interests. So if after all these years and with all the efforts you have put in, you are yet to find your dream job, is it not about time you wake up from your deep slumber? If you cannot find your dream job, then create the job of your dreams as an entrepreneur . Abraham Lincoln said, "The best way to predict the future is to create it". If you have thought along the lines of starting your own business, there are some basic things you must consider before starting your business. Some of these principles may apply generally and also some specific to certain fields.

I have to warn you though, making the leap from employee to entrepreneur means changing not only your lifestyle, but most importantly, your mind-set. Depending on how steeped you are in your old mentality, it may mean a total mental makeover.

And that is what this book is all about. Before spending time, money and energy starting a new business, you should ask yourself: Do I have what it takes to own a business or, am I better suited to being an employee? The answer to the above question should be true and frank to yourself. It was Shakespeare who said, "To thine own self be true". The answer to this question is not finality, but it is a true assessment of the status quo, and when you can rightly deduce your present location, you can take your bearing and chart a course for where you want to be. Those who lie to themselves will self-destruct. Also, those who say, "that's who I am" without giving themselves the allowance to change will end up like the insane - doing the same thing, but expecting a different result.

Here are some questions that might help determine if you have a business owner's mind-set:

1. Can you start and finish tasks independently?

For an employee, the boss or manager gives you a task to be completed within a certain time period and you are expected to complete the assigned task. However, a business owner knows how to, and even likes to, work independently. They are willing to take full responsibility for creating and completing their own work schedules. To take this one step further, if you are thinking about starting a home-based business, you must also consider that there will be times when you'll be spending hours working alone, without the company and support of others. It is important that you realise that not all tasks can wait forever. You have to set your own timelines and deadlines and stick to them without the external supervision of a boss or superior.

2. Can you set and achieve short and long term goals?

As an employee, you are working to achieve someone else's goals and visions. For most people, it is not part of their responsibility to think. They just do as they are told. They will not even take initiative even when the situation throws a curve ball, or something out of the standard operating procedure (SOP) comes up. The business owner takes on the responsibility for initiating, planning, marketing and overseeing the success of their business. Running a successful business means taking the time to formulate and implement a well thought out business plan. You may need to write a concise mission statement, an innovative vision for your company, short and long-term financial goals and a feasible and effective plan of action. Some concerns run without a business plan, but even with a business plan, we all know that things in business rarely go according to plan. It is the responsibility of the business owner to assess present position, relate it to desired destination and do a change of course or strategy as necessary to achieve the desired outcome.

3. Do you have the self-discipline and self-motivation to work for yourself?

For the employee, the boss or manager sets and oversees your tasks and hours. You can do just enough not to get fired. Some work with 'eye service'. They only do what they are told to do when the boss is watching. They have no internal motivation to do their job. They waste time on trivial things or things that do not add any value whatsoever to the business. They are content to just mark time, sign in, sign out and wait for pay day, whether they have made any meaningful contribution to organisational growth or not.

Successful entrepreneurs are masters of time management and multi-tasking. Self-discipline is a vital factor to growing a successful business. A business owner must be consistently self-directed and self-motivated to do those things that will keep his/her business moving forward. Self-discipline is about doing what you say you are going to do when you say you are going to do it, whether you feel like it or not. And there are going to be many days, particularly during business start-up when you are not going to feel like it. Your predicament is compounded by the fact that you are the boss. No one is going to yell at you or give you deadlines or threaten you with a query, your salary or your job. So you need to have the self-discipline and the internal motivation to do what you have to do.

As an entrepreneur, you must continuously evaluate what the most important tasks you have to do on any day are. There are some things you can delegate. Others you can postpone. But there are some tasks that only you can do, and whether they seem urgent or not, you have to do them.

4. Do you understand financial management and can you manage money wisely?

Someone takes all the financial risks for building a successful and profitable business. Employees just earn a salary and they are content to earn and even ask for a raise whether the business is making a profit or not or whether they are making a contribution to the bottom line or not.

But if you decide to start a business, it is a whole different ball game. One of the first thing you must consider is: how do you intend to finance your business? A key factor to starting a business is being prepared to handle the financial ups and downs of opening and growing a new business. Are you willing to take business classes, learn new money management skills and even hire professionals who can help handle your finances? And even when your business is up and running, you must continuously keep a tight leash on financial management. Any slip up will not only affect you and your immediate family, it will affect your employees, your business partners whether suppliers, or creditors alike.

5. Do you know how to measure success?

For some employees, success is equal to a pay check at the end of the month. The boss sets the standard by which they measure and reward your successes – pay raises, awards, recognition, etc. Your call is to meet these minimum standards and you can at least reasonably keep your job. If you exceed such standards or appear to exceed them in your bosses' estimations, you can expect a promotion.

A successful business owner knows almost instinctively how to set his or her own internal and external "barometers of success." As an entrepreneur you are responsible for setting your own standards of excellence. It is important, even before beginning your business, to be fully aware and understand your "barometers of success" and how you professionally measure success. Do you measure success by money earned, recognition received, excellent service delivered, satisfied customers, contribution to society etc.?

6. Are you comfortable creating your own pay check?

As an employee, your employer is responsible for your pay check, benefits and other job related expenses. You can plan on getting paid regularly, and you can plan on how much you will get paid and how your raise or bonuses will come.

However, as a business owner, you are responsible for creating your own pay check, retirement plan, taxes, insurance, vacation pay, etc. There will probably be times when you won't receive a regular pay check. You must think through that and be willing to go through it, if necessary. Being your own boss means taking risks and living with the financial uncertainty that often comes with owning a business. Are you willing to take financial and professional risks? Are you willing to live with the stress that often accompanies an uncertain pay check? Also of extreme importance is the ability to delay gratification. Do you consider a windfall in the business, a sudden surge in income as an invitation to a lavish lifestyle? Or can you still live on your predetermined pay check while you plough back the extra income into building the business or shoring up the finances of the business?

7. Do you know your professional worth?

An employer tells and shows you how much you are worth by the amount they are willing to pay you. It is their valuation of your worth to the organisation or a valuation of what you are bringing to the table.

As a business owner or an entrepreneur, you determine your own worth! And you do not calibrate this self-worth in terms of money. Whatever your account balance is, you know that your self-worth is not tied to your net worth. The recognition of this inherent value inside you, in spite of the apparent results will help pull you through many dark days when even your greatest loyalist will start to question your every step.

8. WI²fm?

"WI²fm" is not a radio station in America, and it is not a radio station in any part of the world for that matter. "WI²fm" is a pertinent question every intending entrepreneur has to answer for himself, by himself. "WI²fm" is an acronym for "What's In It for me". I must say to everyone who cares to hear, home is a long walk from here, and most of the climb is uphill. At a point you will reach a comfortable altitude, but no one can tell when the turbulence will come. You can do everything right and still experience turbulence, it just comes with the territory.

Some people go into business with the sole aim of making money. The essence of entrepreneurship is to make a meaning, make a difference or make the world a better place. If you make meaning, you will probably make money. But if you set out to make money, you may end up not making both. Your motivation must be to improve the value of life, right a wrong or make sure that something good is preserved. You must decide before you set out what ends you desire from the venture.

You must take off properly and navigate the course well to land at your predetermined destination. You must define your own success, and make the journey itself an integral part of your success story. People are going to play a major part in the journey, you cannot go it alone, but the whole journey has to be fulfilling an inner desire inside you. Your personal fulfilment must be satisfied, in part, by what you achieve or else all the accolades and achievement will be hollow and meaningless. Your definition of personal success must transcend money or the things money can buy. You must determine before you set out whether achieving success in your chosen endeavour will fulfil your inner desires.

9. Do you have the Power?

Passion is the fuel that keeps people burning with that unquenchable zeal when they meet the many obstacles that every business meets time and again. Passion is what keeps you going when no else can see why you are still headed in that direction.

If you lose the passion, you lose the power. As a leader, your people can sense your passion for what you are doing. If you have enough genuine passion for what you are doing, it will rub off on some of them. When a leader lacks conviction, his people will lose commitment to the cause.

10. All over or all over again?

A high percentage of start-up businesses fail. Even with the best business plan, best advice, careful planning and execution, many businesses still do fail. Sometimes, a post mortem can clearly reveal the reason why the business failed. At other times, it may be circumstances beyond the control of the business owner like sudden change in government regulation or like the case of wars or natural disasters. If you start a business and it fails, then what?

You must learn to separate yourself as a person from your business. This is where the value of inherent self-worth that we looked at earlier is very critical. Your business may have failed, that is an event, but you are not a failure. You must be willing to start "all over again" instead of giving up and saying "it's all over".

Success is going from failure to failure without losing enthusiasm. You will learn a lot more from your failure than from your success. Nothing teaches like the school of hard knocks. I think the world is doing itself some great disservice by not learning from all the failures that abound around us. We all try to learn from successful people, trying to learn what they did that made them successful. Some of them have let us down by sincerely telling us that they are not sure what exactly they did that got them where they are called successful today. But failures too could teach us some vital lessons, for from some people you learn what to do, and from others, you learn what not to do.

Even if your business fails, know that it is not over till it is over. It is not over till you quit. You are not a failure till you quit. You just have learned like Thomas Edison, one way of not starting a business, and who knows, the next time you try, you just might be the next start up success story like the many that abound.

If you start a business and lose all your money, it is not all lost, except if you did not learn anything from the experience. Consider the money as tuition in the school of hard knocks, the University of Life, for which the textbooks, hand outs or manuals do not immune you from failure or perfect you without practice, but everything is learned hands-on, DIY.

11. Do you have a good appetite for problems?

There are many good reasons why most employees will never start their business, or venture to work for themselves. Most people's fear of failure overpowers their desire for success and some people are averse to problems. Entrepreneurship in the purest sense is an open invitation to solve problems. Employees learn how to refer problems to their boss. Even if they can stretch themselves and deal with the situation, they pass the buck. An entrepreneur is akin to the American president who said, "The buck stops here".

A famous quote says that "Problems are the breakfast of champions." You get promoted for every challenge you pass through. No matter how bad a challenge is, if it does not kill you, it will make you stronger. Your reward is commensurate to the problems you solve. Someone said there is no mystery to money; money is a reward for solving problems. A simple business model that has created millionaires over and over again is: find a problem, solve it better than anyone else, solve it for as many people as you can, and you can go smiling to the bank.

"Entrepreneurship is neither a science nor an art. It is a practice."

– Peter Drucker

Chapter Thirteen

VIP ONLY

People are your greatest asset and at the same time your greatest challenge. The hardest decisions companies have to make have to do with people. You have to deal with hiring, firing, promoting, redeploying and many other things in between.

I have seen many books about starting your own business. People advocate many different things in these books. Some of these books are written by people who have no business writing business books because they have never been in business for themselves. They want to give comforting advice to you for a shoe that they have never worn and send you on a wild goose chase on a trail they have never travelled on.

THE ENTREPRENEUR

When I talk with people who want to start a business, they often tell me that their greatest inhibition is capital, and I have tried many times with little success to convince them otherwise.

Starting a business has never been easier and cheaper than it is today. You can have all the capital in the word and put it into your business and it still would amount to nothing if the most important variable is not in place. I have also heard the myth of the prodigious idea. So many people go around waiting for one big idea to hit them in the head like an apple falling from a tree, so that they can start running. But there have been many great businesses built around ideas that have been here forever. If you get the big idea, good, but there have been many failed businesses with what seemed like great ideas.

"Nothing is everything." So there is not one attribute, character trait or factor that can determine the success or failure of a business. Yet, all the factors do not have equal impact on the success or failure of a business.

Of all the factors of production, the human capital is the most important single determinant of the fate of a business entity. People will make or break your business. They will cause your ship to sink or sail. And the primus inter pares is the entrepreneur. He is the initiator, motivator, leader, strategist... many things rolled into one person.

Everything rises and falls on leadership. A leader sets the tone for his organisation. And when it comes to building organisational culture, people take their bearing from the leader. Thus the most important person in a business venture is the entrepreneur. He is the leader of the army, even though sometimes it is an army of one.

Most people view leadership from the perspective of what the leaders do without looking at who the leader is. His actions are like fruits but the root of these actions and choices are more deep seated. It is the unchangeable core of who the leader is which determines what he does even when it seems like it is on a whim. The character, strong sense of purpose and calm in the midst of the storm helps the leader to navigate the many concourses of leadership.

A business can only grow as far as the entrepreneur grows. Jim Rohn says it best, "Income rarely exceeds personal development." Sometimes income can take a lucky jump, but if you do not rise to meet it, income will shrink back down to where you are.

The best money you will ever invest is the money you invest in your personal development. Dedicate yourself to the learning process. If you do, I can promise you that your life will always be on an upward trajectory. Invest in books, DVDs, webinars, seminars etc. Personal development cannot be outsourced. A recent survey said that the average American reads one book a year, but the average CEO reads five books a month. Are you still wondering why one is average and the other is the CEO? They say, "Readers are Leaders".

STAFF

One of my strategies for investment in any business is that, I will not invest in a business enterprise that does not have infinite possibilities for growth. I do not mind a small start-up, but I do not want to start a small business that will remain a midget forever. And in order for a business to grow, you must bring in staff members, you cannot do it all by yourself. There are some responsibilities that you can never outsource but if you want to have a hand in all the pies, you will remain small forever.

Staffing is a way to multiply your effort and achieve quantum return on your idea. You can duplicate yourself in multiple places by employing other people.

When it comes to hiring, most people go for people with proven track record as they call it, experience or multiple degrees from Ivy League schools. For a start-up, you may not be able to hire this calibre of staff and some may not be willing to join a start-up with an uncertain future. You will do better with someone who is in love with your business and will be your evangelist. This is more important than their degrees.

For a start-up, hire people you can work with. Because the number of staff is low, you are not just creating a team, you are creating a family. And if you hire the wrong people, you will create a dysfunctional family.

Hire people better than you and put their brains to work. I saw a book recently titled "Why A students work for D students". So even if you are a D student, hire the A students. And when it comes to areas where their strength surpasses yours, be willing to get yourself and your ego out of the way and give them a chance to contribute to the advancement of the enterprise.

CUSTOMERS

The people who said "The customer is always right" got it wrong somewhat. I am more attuned with those who said "The customer is king". You must treat your customers like kings and queens, and even if the king is wrong, you must tell his majesty like a king. No matter how good your staff members are and how dumb your competitors are, customers are the ones that will determine whether you stay in business or you join the un-ending list of those who get dumped on the scrap heap of failed businesses.

One thing that can set your business apart and keep you miles ahead of the competition is how you treat your customers. Most people have some sentimental attachment to their money and if they have to part with it, they are very concerned not just with what they are getting but who they are giving the money to and how they feel about the whole process. You can offer the same or a better product at a lower price to a customer and if it just "does not feel right" with the customer, they will not do business with you or will never do repeat business with you. There are some nuances you will never get your hand on when it comes to customer satisfaction, but you have to do everything you can to serve the customer as king. Quality product or service should never be compromised, no matter the cost to you.

COMPETITORS

Competitors are an integral part of the business terrain. It will be nice not to have competition, but the business terrain makes room for competition. It will be an unfair advantage for any company to perpetually have the sole monopoly of some product or service. In certain instances, it will be a breach of anti-trust laws, and the penalty is severe for defaulters. Companies have been fined multi-million dollars for cases of unfair competition.

Given that competitors are a part of the business terrain, you must devise strategies to use them to your advantage. Not only must you know what your competitors have in the market, you must try to know what they are planning to bring to the market. Otherwise, when they blind side you, you can lose a major part of your market share and it could take forever to regain the lost market share.

Replicating what your competition is doing is a sure bet way to play second fiddle. You must offer a unique advantage to your customers that your competition cannot replicate easily. It may be excellent product, unrivalled customer experience, convenience in doing business with you, money back guarantees... or any other offering that make you stand out from the crowd.

PARTNERSHIPS

When you hear Steve Jobs, you think "Apple", Bill Gates, "Microsoft", Mark Zuckerberg, "Facebook", Richard Branson, "Virgin" and the list goes on and on. Most successful companies have a name that is synonymous with them. A critical element often downplayed is that these entrepreneurs were not lone rangers or solo players. There were other people without whom the story would have been different. They were not self-made in the sense of the word. Each of them had partners, friends, a team or mentors that made their dream possible.

The success of the enterprise is often attributed to the CEO, but strategic partnerships and alliances helped to bring the CEO's dream to reality. They say that two heads are better than one, and it works for an entrepreneur because no one has it all. Each individual has his talents, strength and weaknesses. It can get pretty lonely working on your own, and many hands make the work lighter. One of the most important strategic moves you can make in building an organisation is building a team. With a good team, everything does not rest on you. Even in your absence, the work can still go on and you can delegate some things so that you can focus on the more critical tasks.

You must exercise utmost caution when going into partnerships. Many businesses have met their waterloo because of partnerships that did not work. The more you know the person, the better for you. There is no easy template or algorithm to choose who you should partner with. Sometimes, you must make this decision at gut level. That is why an entrepreneur must have discernment.

GOOD COMPANY

Do not be misled: "Bad Company corrupts good character." 1 Cor. 15:33 (NIV)

We are creatures who crave community. Even God said in Genesis that "it is not good for man to be alone". Yet, it is better to be alone than to be in bad company. As much as we desire to associate, we must watch the company we keep. Peer pressure is not only a problem for teenagers. If we stay long enough in the wrong company, we cannot effectively immune ourselves from their influence in the long run. We may act tough like we are not being influenced, but why dissipate energy resisting the negative influence when you can change your company and put yourself under positive influence instead.

There are people who just being around them makes you better. There are others who are so toxic that you should avoid them like a plague. No wonder someone said "bad attitude is so contagious; it should be labelled a disease." Pessimists are a pest. You become like the people you spend the most time with. It may start subtly, the changes will not be noticeable at first, but after a while, you learn their language, their ways and become like them.

Your net worth is a reflection of your network. You are the average of your ten closest friends. Someone said "If you are the tenth friend of nine broke people, you will soon be the tenth broke guy".

Keep company with wise people and you will become wiser. Keep company with people richer, wiser and smarter than you. If you are the smartest person in a room, then you are in the wrong room. Keep company with people who intimidate you in some way. Draw inspiration from them and aspire to higher heights. Do not become the one eyed man in the city of the blind. Keep company with those who uplift you, whose presence brings out your best.

The biggest barrier to happiness is associating with miserable and angry people. Hurting people hurt people. Misery loves and needs company. Miserable people want to make others in their image. Surround yourself with happy people and you will be happy.

"If you hang out with chickens, you're going to cluck and if you hang out with eagles, you're going to fly." Do not hang out with people busy doing nothing or if you see people who are going nowhere, do not go with them.

Avoid time wasters. Avoid people who do not respect your time, because they do not respect your life. Remember, your time is your life.

Do not choose friends based solely on common past or shared experiences. Rather, choose your friends based on a common future. As you grow, your friendship should change, cut off negative or toxic associations and develop new ones.

BE YOUR OWN BOSS?

One of the greatest fascinations of going into business for yourself apart from the financial returns is the popular prospect of "being your own boss".

This is certainly a very exciting benefit of working for yourself, but are you really your own boss? Some people see being their own boss as the ultimate freedom. They envisage a situation where they answer to no one and do not have to take instruction from anybody or defer to anyone. Nothing could be further from the truth. As a serial entrepreneur, I can tell you from experience that when you go into business for yourself, you realise that you just traded one boss, for many.

First, you are your own boss, so you will answer to yourself, so whether you are a bad boss or not, you will answer to yourself. Then comes the scary part; you may have had one direct boss before but now, you are suddenly thrust into a field where you have many bosses with staggering needs, demands and deadlines that must all be met yesterday. Welcome to entrepreneurship, where every client no matter how small they are is your boss in more ways than one. We said earlier that the customer is king, and in this regard, they are your boss, and you must treat them as such or you will lose them.

"The best things in life are not things but people."
                                                    Art Buchwald.

Chapter Fourteen

COMMON MISTAKES
ENTERPRENEURS MAKE

"A person who never made a mistake never tried anything new."

Albert Einstein

Going into business for almost any reason is a good reason if you do it right. The reason you choose to go into business is not nearly as important as doing it right and avoiding the many pitfalls many businesses fall into.

Available data shows that as many as one out of ten start-ups fail within the first few years. Those are not very good odds but if you can anticipate and plan for the pitfalls, crags, quick sand and the many perils that lie in wait for a business, you increase your chances of becoming one of the success stories of entrepreneurship. Mistakes are inevitable, but you don't have to make the same ones everyone else does and you do not have to make the same mistakes over and over again.

1. The launch: Too Early or Too Late?

It is hard to generalize when it is perfect to start a business. Reid Hoffman, co-founder of LinkedIn said, "If you're not embarrassed by the first version of your product, you've launched too late". Starting too early may be a problem but it is better than starting late which is as much a problem as not starting at all. Even if you are not sure that what you are offering is ready for the market and the market is ready for it, you can lead the market and fix the bugs, learn from your mistakes as you go along. An example is the personal computer market. The market was not asking for personal computers, people did not even know they needed one, but when the product hit the shelves, the market caught on. And till this very day, many years on, the personal computer market is still under continuous innovation. Software updates come time and again. Hard wares are continuously undergoing redesign, to fix problems with previous versions or increase customer experience. Trying to do things serially instead of concurrently can also pose a major problem. You should initiate Parallel processes where multiple things are moving down the road at the same time. This may entail juggling multiple balls and doing the balancing act of making sure no one falls down. Even if you drop the ball, pick it up and go on.

2. To Quit Or Not To Quit

The tale of entrepreneurs is replete with stories of people who tried countless times before succeeding at the quest. Motivation is like steady vitamin supplement for entrepreneurs. What they often do not tell us are stories of the many perennial failures that litter the business landscape. What is the use of flogging a dead horse or burying a living one? To quit and when to quit or to keep at it, is a case by case call. View your situation critically, assess yourself and your venture unapologetically, do not lie to yourself or your partners or investors, do not make faulty assumptions, and do not ignore critical facts in deciding whether you should quit or carry on. If you quit a particular venture, you can take the lessons learnt and use them in your next venture. Quitting should be like "He who fights and run away" living to fight another day, instead of dying on the battle field.

3. Loving The Method More Than The Result

Many business plans and models form the casket in which some businesses are buried. Some people are so emotionally and romantically in love with their business model that they take their eyes off the goal. They fall in love with methods and processes, and even if they are not working, they refuse to change them in line with the predetermined goals. Results cannot be mortgaged for methods. A similar problem is getting stuck on a business idea that has no possibility of success. There is no guarantee that any new idea will succeed, but some ideas are dead on arrival and the earlier you bury the carcass and move on to better things, the better for everyone.

Every business plan or projection is based on certain assumptions. Believing your assumptions over field experience or prevailing results, refusing to change what is not working will spell doom for any enterprise.

4. Much Ado About Money?

Most people do not go into business for the money. That is a noble thing to do. Any successful business will make money except it is a humanitarian organization. Some entrepreneurs ignore the financial side of their business. The hard truth is that you may not be in it for the money but without the money you will not be in it at all. Even if you grow to a level where you have a Chief Financial Officer (CFO), never forgot to check the books. They say the devil is in the details, so check the details. You cannot but know the state of your bottom line. Money is the life blood of the company. No matter how big you grow, you must control cost, plug leaks, sell and maximize return on investment. If you fail at managing the money, you will fail in business altogether.

5. I Am Not A Sales Man

One of the attributes of an entrepreneur is multitasking, dynamism and versatility. Right from the start or when your business has reached a certain stage, you can delegate some tasks and expect that they will be done and done well. But, you can never stop selling. You are the "chief evangelist" of the organization (borrowing a phrase from Guy Kawasaki). For small start-ups, the entrepreneur is everything and also the sales man. No matter what label you choose to wear down the road, never stop selling. None of your team will boast of the same circle of contacts as you, so take advantage of your influence and advance the course of the company. If you are too big to sell, then you are too big not to fail.

6. Get Rich Quick

Entrepreneurship is not a get rich quick scheme. If you get a business proposal that promises like a get rich quick scheme, get out of there quick. Entrepreneurship is about going the long haul. I remember the dotcom era where it was like you could get rich and retire in ten seconds. Those kinds of dreams usually end in nightmares. Do not be overly optimistic in estimating the break-even point particularly if there are investors. It is better to under-promise and over deliver than over promise and under-deliver.

7. Unhealthy Competition

For me, you can compete across many broad spectrums with others in the same line of business. To reduce your competition to a price war is an unhealthy competition. The problem is that every other person can compete on that term easily. It is not rocket science and it requires no complex algorithm to implement. You can become a game changer by shifting competition to other spheres like a unique business model, delivering top quality, excellent customer service, un-matched speed of delivery, convenience of ordering and paying for your product or service, better after sales service, money back guarantee and other things that your competition cannot easily replicate.

8. Poor Customer Service Or Poor Quality Service/Product

A business model that aims to serve customers only once and does not engender repeat customers and referrals will soon run out of new customers and then go out of business. Repeat customers will guarantee you longevity and income stability in business and they can become for you free advertisement to their circle. It is a debilitating mistake to give poor quality service or product. Under promise and over deliver, whatever the cost. Like we have said, the customer may not always be right, but treat them like they are kings.

9. Unethical Practices

Rather fail doing it right than succeed doing it the wrong way. Do not deal underhand with your customers or with the government. Stay on the right side of the law. Obtain necessary permits and pay requisite practicing fees or levies. If you break the law, you are definitely setting yourself up for the authorities to shut down your operations and they may proceed to prosecute you. Ignorance is no defence; it is your duty to know the guiding laws surrounding your industry. Do not defraud your suppliers or sub-contractors, word goes round fast and you may not be able to experience any concession they would have extended to you and in some cases, they may black list you completely.

10. Scaling: Sooner or Later?

Just as the case of "To Quit Or Not To Quit" it is hard to generalize when a business is ready to scale. Different set-ups have different prerequisites for scaling. As a general rule of thumb, it is safer to scale too slow than to scale too soon. If you open up branches all over the place, hire sales and marketing teams, buy and brand cars based on optimistic projections, it will amount to serious drain on company finances if either the market or production does not match up with the expanded operations. It is better that you scale gradually and as close to the production capacity and market indices as possible. Know the size of your target market and whether it is shrinking or growing and know the rate of growth or shrinkage. Know your market share and also the rate and direction of growth. Scaling is usually based on an optimistic expectation of growth of your market share or entire target market. If you scale and fall short of the target a couple of times, the company can go under, dragged down by its own weight or even your investors can pull the plug on you.

11. Other People's Money (OPM)

Most start-ups get money from venture capitalists or angel investors to fund their enterprise. Even if you retain 51% of the shares for control reasons, you will still lose control of the organization once you take investors' money. Most board decisions do not come down to a vote, so your 51% stake will sometimes not do you any good. Even though your venture capitalist will tell you that they believe in you and they invested in you, if the figures are not adding up properly, they will wield the big stick. If you can run your start-up without sourcing capital, the better.

12. Hire and Fire

People will make or break your business. You may not be in control of your customers or investors. But when it comes to hiring, you should have a say on who comes on board your ship. One ground rule says, "hire slow, fire fast". If you put up with bad staff members for too long, they can do your outfit extensive and irreparable damage. Another rule is "do not hire someone you cannot fire". For some people, that may mean do not hire your childhood friend, your wife's brother, your partner's siblings and the likes. The connections are too surreal to engender good working relationship most of the time.

Hiring like-endowed persons instead of likeminded persons is another hiring mistake. Do not fill the organization with people just like you. Hire people who complement your skill. Balance the skill sets in the company.

Another grave mistake is confusing friendship with business relationships, particularly with your investors. In your life, know what everybody is in for and what is in it for everybody. Do not expect business relationships to fulfil some friendship needs.

Do not be obsessed about partnering. There are too many variables that you need to clarify before you sign a pact with anybody. Rather pay more for less temporarily, than be permanently hitched with the wrong wagon. It can drag your brand, your name, business integrity and then your business to the ground.

13. Waiting For Perfect Practice

Taking massive action is sometimes the difference between success and failure. Spending all your time perfecting pitches, business plans, or brochures instead of focusing on delivering the product or prototype is a costly mistake. People will do business with you even if you do not have a bespoke business plan, amazing brochures, interactive and responsive website, if you can deliver the goods. We were told that "anything worth doing is worth doing well" but that is if you can do it well. Les brown said "anything worth doing is worth doing badly till you start doing it well". So get to doing, the miracle is in the doing.

14. Prisoner of Conscience

One trap that any entrepreneur should never fall into is the résumé or past experience trap. You must reserve the ability to reinvent yourself multiple times if necessary on the road to success. Do not let your resume or experience dictate who you are. You must learn to evaluate what you are doing, hold fast to what works, work it some more, but be bold enough to discard what is not working and try your hands on something new or try it in a new way.

Many opportunities will come to you that will be out of your immediate area of concentration or the things that you have done before. You cannot pass up those opportunities because it does not fit smugly into your résumé. You must take those opportunities to grow as a person or a business. Take the brief, go to work on whatever it is and even if you are not going to take the offer, do not make the call instantly. The best thing about this is that if you take the new opportunity, you learn how to do a job in the new area with the promise of repeat business from the same company or others and also, once you have done a job for a company, you become an inside person and that puts you in line for more jobs in the same or other areas with the company.

You must get out of your résumé or your past and create and take advantages of opportunities as they come. When the business environment throws you a curve ball, you must always find ways to say yes. No matter what it says on your card, brochure or website, you should be willing to take some uncharted paths, particularly when the charted terrain is taking you nowhere twice as fast.

15. Nothing is Everything

Fads come and go, principles stay for ever. Continuously being tossed by changing fads in disregard for timeless principles is a grave error. Consistency is one of the hallmarks of a good entrepreneur. Your moral compass should not be set in relation to the fad of the day. It is a serious mistake to ignore principles and follow fads.

The success or failure of a business is a culmination of many factors. It is sometimes a delicate balancing act. It is like a system that is made up of many parts. Focusing on a certain aspect of the life of the company while ignoring others, may create a lopsided growth which can hinder the full realisation of organisational potential. Everything is a combination of many things and each of the components must be properly juxtaposed and functional to create an efficient system.

16. Self-Made Or Self-Un-Made

Entrepreneurship may mean running your own gig on your own terms, but the best way to shorten your learning curve and achieve a specific result is to find people who have already achieved what you want and then model their behaviour. Rather than try to figure it all out on your own, find someone who has already achieved what you want, determine how this person did it, model this behaviour and make it your own.

While you might seek a relationship with a face-to-face human mentor, you could also hire a coach, read a book or articles by an expert or do web research. After some consideration, you may decide what steps to take to realise your own dreams. You do not have all the time and money to make all the mistakes there are to make. Convert the experience of others to avoidable mistakes. You will make enough mistakes by yourself, so avoid all the ones you can.

17. Count The Cost

"Is there anyone here who, planning to build a new house, doesn't first sit down and figure the cost so you'll know if you can complete it? If you only get the foundation laid and then run out of money, you're going to look pretty foolish. Everyone passing by will poke fun at you. He started something he couldn't finish." (Luke 14:28-30: The Message Version)

The bible sums up this costly mistake succinctly. The entrepreneur is very often an optimistic person and this optimism is reflected in his business projections. If you focus on the returns without adequately factoring in the cost of running the business apart from the start-up cost, you can run out of money and the business can go under for that reason. Adequate research is a serious prerequisite before getting into any venture. Even after the research, you must allow some money for unforeseen expenses that may come up.

When you are projecting the break-even time for the company, it is better to be more conservative than optimistic. It does you a lot better if you break-even before the target date, than run short of your projections. As we say "under promise, over deliver"

18. Winking In The Dark

Have you ever bought a good product and then wondered why the product is not all over the place? Or have you ever seen someone render you a service and marvel at how good they are, yet nobody knows. Advertising can make the difference between success and failure for a business. No matter how good you

WHY I FIRED MY BOSS

are or how good your product is, if people do not know you or know your product, they will not buy.

For large corporations, advertising budget is a major chunk of their expenditure. But the advent of social media has created an almost free platform for you to reach countless numbers of people. With Facebook, Twitter, Instagram and other social media platforms, you can reach so many people on a shoe string budget.

You can be in people's faces, by way of advertising, but make sure that they recognize your brand for good and associate it with quality and service delivery. Aggressive advertising may promote a mediocre product but discerning customers will only fall for the trick once.

This list is by no means exhaustive. There are more mistakes countless entrepreneurs have made and will make again. This is just a small guide to common mistakes, so that you do not repeat them. There will be more mistakes to be made out there, but that is not reason enough not to venture into entrepreneurship. In this business, sometimes you win, sometimes, you learn.

I have not failed. I've just found 10,000 ways that won't work."

Thomas Edison

Chapter Fifteen

NEW WORLD ORDER

"You do not need a digital strategy. You need a marketing strategy for the digital age."

Judy Goldberg, Sony Pictures.

Peter Drucker said that these are the times of the three Cs: "Accelerated Change, tremendous Competition and overwhelming Complexity". The world as we know it is changing at such a rate that a blink of an eye can give you culture shock. Keeping up with the dizzying speed of change can be breath taking. But to be competitive in this business world, you do not just have to be in touch with time, you have to be at the cutting edge and if you can, lead the change.

Technology has completely revolutionised how we do everything. Looking at the future, there are a few areas that we must consider and they will play significant roles in determining the shape of things to come.

Globalization has somehow reduced the life span of mega-businesses and opened a plethora of opportunity for small start-ups. Though it is a time of huge opportunities for entrepreneurs, we must understand the shifts that are taking place in our world to take advantage of them.

Some of the areas that are engendering these shifts include:

DIGITALIZATION

The Information Age has affected the workforce in that automation, digitalization and computerization of almost everything has resulted in higher productivity but in many places coupled with net job loss. The digital industry creates a knowledge-based society in a high-tech global economy that increases efficiency and convenience in manufacturing throughput and service sector operation.

One indispensable attribute of those who want to thrive in the digital age is lifelong learning. You must be willing to continuously evolve and reinvent yourself and your company as time goes on. You cannot build a monument to what used to work.

We are in a new day and age and it is not a temporary shift but a permanent change in the way our global economy functions, and this new age demands a new mind-set.

GLOBALIZATION

The changes we are seeing in our world are not only historic but unprecedented in so many different spheres. Urbanisation is happening in many cities across the globe. Rural-urban migration is as constant as the pull of gravity.

Globalization is one of those phenomena that seem to have happened on the world. We just woke up one day and realised that by the way we interact and do business now, the peoples of the world are incorporated into a single world society. Virtually nothing is "local trouble" anymore.

There was a time when the competition in any industry was within the same geographical location. Then with the advent of telephone, rail transport and aeroplanes, the competition took a national scale. But since the advent of the internet, international borders have been virtually obliterated and the competition has simply gone global. The competition is not down the block or round the bend, on the next street or across the city; it is just a few clicks away.

You can now order anything, from anywhere on the globe all from the comfort of your home or even from your hand held devices. In a similar vein, you can sell your product or service virtually everywhere on the globe. Potentially, your reach is global but your grasp is determined by your scope.

Globalization is no longer a concept; it is a present day reality. Things that happen in any country can have effect on the economies of other countries almost instantly. No one is immune from the market ups and downs of other countries. The world economy is so interconnected that untangling the sinuous links is virtually impossible. "No man is an island" and now no nation is either.

VIRTUAL REALITY

At the height of its growth, Kodak had about 145,000 employees. Instagram when it sold for about a Billion dollars had only 13 employees! Welcome to the new world. Size is not might and might is not right, necessarily. Even production plants are getting smaller. Most jobs that were manually done are now being handled by robots and computer aided manufacturing. There will always be factories that will produce tangible goods. The reality of the new world is that there are many businesses with no assets in the sense of factories, and no bogus staff list yet they are worth staggering sums. A case in point, Uber is an app-based transportation network and taxi company, headquartered in San Francisco, California, which operates in cities in many countries. Uber is one of the fastest growing businesses in the world today. Uber is essentially a Mobile App (a computer program, using a cell phone), which makes it possible for you to call a "taxi". Uber does not own the taxis nor cars of its own, yet Uber is valued at around 40 Billion dollars. Amazon is worth over 30 Billion dollars. We have Facebook, twitter, Google and so many other tech companies with staggering net worth.

In this virtual reality, there is no need for extensive capital outlay, physical infrastructure or bogus staff ensemble to run a profitable venture. This has greatly helped in reducing the start-up costs for entrepreneurs. You do not have to have a real office or think of staff and other overhead to be in business. As we have seen in many cases such as that of Mark Zuckerberg and Facebook, it now seems possible for a group of relatively inexperienced people with limited capital to take advantage of the opportunities offered by the information age to succeed on a large scale.

In a virtual business model, there are no fixed hierarchies in the organisations like pyramid corporations. What we will see are free flowing project teams, small units like independent contractors yet delivering cutting edge services and products and gaining value in the market place.

24-7

The days of nine-to-five or the forty hour work week are over. The earlier we all realise that, the better. Gone are the days when life was compartmentalised. There was work time or work days and there was play time. Now, every day is a work day and every day is a play day. The world will not wait for you or stick to your little bitty time schedule. With the proliferation of smart phones, tablets, the internet, virtual offices, people can work from just about anywhere. And with the interconnectedness of the world, there is always somebody somewhere who is available to render whatever service you desire round the clock.

The new reality is "online real time" with no down time. The world is like a perpetual wheel turning and churning out results round the clock. In the age we live in, your business is either online or you are out of line and will soon be out of business.

LIFE-LONG LEARNING

Another dimension of the new world order is life time education or retooling as they call it in some places. Whatever qualification or skill you come to the market place with, you must stay in touch with current trends and shifts. You will not only need to re-invent your business model but also re-invent yourself to stay relevant. When you walk out of a university, or an MBA, you cannot pack your books into a case and say au revoir to learning. The shift around you will leave you in a maze in no time.

The market place will always discipline people who are not prepared first of all and then those who are stuck in the past and who are not prepared to change with time and tide. According to Sulley Breaks, these are people who are "reluctant to change, function the same with nothing to gain".

Principles are constant but times are changing. The only people who will not just survive but thrive in these changing times are those who understand and change with the changing times.

Welcome to the new world.

This Is Not The End. It Is Not Even The Beginning Of The End. But It Is Perhaps, The End Of The Beginning.

Winston S. Churchill

www.ingramcontent.com/pod-product-compliance
Lightning Source LLC
Chambersburg PA
CBHW071426180526
45170CB00001B/239